AF725002

Doing Well by Doing Good

Innovative Corporate Responses to Communicable Diseases

Copyediting by Kimberly Gould Ashizawa.
Cover design and typographic design by Patrick Ishiyama.

Cover photographs
Left: Awareness-raising session for construction workers in Vietnam (photo by JCIE)
Right: A factory producing mosquito nets (photo provided by Sumitomo Chemical)

Printed in Japan.
ISBN 978-4-88907-081-1

Japan Center for International Exchange
4-9-17 Minami Azabu, Minato-ku, Tokyo 106-0047 Japan
URL: www.jcie.or.jp

Japan Center for International Exchange, Inc. (JCIE/USA)
274 Madison Avenue, Suite 1102, New York NY 10016 USA
URL: www.jcie.org

Table of Contents

Contributors

Susan Hubbard, Senior Associate, Japan Center for International Exchange, New York (JCIE/USA)

Communicable Diseases and the Corporate Sector
Bayer China
Standard Chartered Bank
Levi Strauss and Company (co-authored)
M·A·C Cosmetics
MTV

Satoko Itoh, Chief Program Officer, Japan Center for International Exchange, Tokyo (JCIE)

Coca-Cola Company
Sumitomo Chemical
Toyota South Africa Motors
Central Azucarera Don Pedro (co-authored)

Tomoko Suzuki, Senior Program Officer, JCIE

Anglo American
DaimlerChrysler South Africa

Tomone Kozen, Program Officer, JCIE

Central Azucarera Don Pedro (co-authored)
Taisei Construction Corporation
Levi Strauss and Company (co-authored)

Translation and research assistance:

Sachiko Aoki, Program Associate, JCIE
David Monico, Program Associate, JCIE/USA

Note: The majority of the research and interviews for this project were conducted in 2006 and 2007. Some of the cases were updated since then with publicly available information, but unless otherwise stated, information should be considered current as of 2007. All efforts were made to confirm the accuracy of the contents with the companies in question in 2007, but any inaccuracies remain the responsibility of JCIE.

Foreword

The idea for a global funding mechanism to drive the fight against the major communicable diseases was first discussed at the Kyushu-Okinawa G8 Summit in Japan in 2000, and the Global Fund to Fight AIDS, Tuberculosis and Malaria (the Global Fund) was created two years later in 2002. The Global Fund later approached the Japan Center for International Exchange (JCIE) with the idea of creating a private support group to raise awareness in Japan about communicable diseases and the role of the Global Fund and to encourage stronger commitments from all sectors of society in Japan to the fight against communicable diseases. Following that discussion, the Friends of the Global Fund, Japan (FGFJ), was born in 2004.

In addition to its efforts to increase the Japanese government's financial contributions to the Global Fund, the FGFJ encourages Japanese companies to find creative ways to engage in the fight against communicable diseases. Several companies in Japan were already playing important roles in the fight before the FGFJ was launched, and some of their experiences are described in this volume. But, in order to find other examples of the myriad ways in which corporate engagement can contribute to stemming the spread and impact of communicable diseases, as well as contribute to the corporation's bottom line, the FGFJ decided to collect examples of successful cases from around the world.

A growing number of Japanese companies are expressing interest in engaging in the fight against communicable diseases, but they have reported that they do not know how to go about doing so. They are concerned that there might be a backlash against them for getting involved in controversial issues, particularly when dealing with HIV/AIDS, and executives are looking for the tools to convince their superiors of the importance of corporate engagement even in diseases that are not necessarily contracted in the workplace. In an attempt to respond to these concerns, the FGFJ research team chose to focus the case studies primarily on decision-making processes and the ways in which companies have dealt with the challenges that inevitably emerge, as well as the impact of their activities both on the state of communicable diseases in their target communities and on the companies themselves.

Earlier drafts of these case studies were discussed at a February 5, 2007, FGFJ symposium in Tokyo on "Corporate Responses to Communicable Diseases" and a roundtable on "Partnerships for Fighting Communicable Diseases" the following day, which were organized in cooperation with the Global Business Coalition on HIV/AIDS, Tuberculosis and Malaria (GBC) and the Nippon Keidanren (Japan Business Federation).

Working with the GBC and the Nippon Keidanren, the FGFJ identified 12 companies that have successfully developed and implemented programs to fight the spread of HIV/AIDS, tuberculosis, and malaria. This is by no means meant to be an exhaustive list of corporations that are playing an important role in this fight. Rather, it is merely a sampling of companies that represent a broad range of industries, sizes, and geographic locations. They vary widely in terms of the kinds of activities they engage in and the approaches they take. Two things that the cases all have in common, however, is strong leadership at some level and partnership with other sectors, and those themes are discussed in depth in the case studies and analyses in this volume.

The research team conducted interviews with top leadership in the target companies as well as with the people who were responsible for implementing activities. Where possible, they also spoke with some of the companies' government and NGO partners. The team also spoke in-depth with several intermediary organizations that help companies design their programs and facilitate cross-sectoral partnership and learning.

I would like to thank, on behalf of the research team, all those corporate leaders, NGO representatives, and government officials who took the time to meet with our team, offer feedback on draft chapters, and engage in an ongoing dialogue with the FGFJ on this important field of corporate engagement in the fight against communicable diseases. Everyone involved in the cases presented in this book has taken brave, bold steps to help save lives in their own communities and around the world, and we appreciate your taking time out of your busy schedules to share that experience with us. I would also like to thank the Bill and Melinda Gates Foundation, the Open Society Institute, and the United Nations Foundation for their generous support of the FGFJ over the years. Finally, I offer my gratitude to Kimberly Gould Ashizawa of JCIE for copyediting this report and Patrick Ishiyama, also of JCIE, for the layout and design.

I sincerely hope that the cases presented in this volume will continue to spark ideas in the minds of corporate leaders in Japan and elsewhere as we continue to look for ways to work together in this shared fight against communicable diseases.

Tadashi Yamamoto
President, JCIE
Director, FGFJ

Communicable Diseases and the Corporate Sector

As globalization continues to bring people from around the world closer together, more and more attention is being paid to the global challenge of communicable diseases. In the past two decades, AIDS has grown to become one of the most destructive epidemics in recorded history, and billions of dollars have been poured into reducing the spread of HIV infection—the virus that causes AIDS—and prolonging and improving the quality of life of those already infected. Despite the fact that malaria has been eradicated in the world's advanced industrialized countries, it is still a major threat to communities in much of the developing world, where it is among the major causes of mortality among children under the age of five. We are now witnessing a renewed drive to combat—and even eradicate—malaria by a variety of actors around the world. On top of all of this, we have been forced to come to a gradual recognition that a third major communicable disease—tuberculosis—is still a serious concern in modern times, and the increase in frequency and severity of drug-resistant strains, as well as the respiratory infection's ability to travel anywhere in the world, have made it a significant global threat, prompting urgent new efforts to combat its spread.

In 2000, the international community agreed to a set of basic goals—the Millennium Development Goals (MDGs)—for achieving minimum standards of life, livelihood, health, and equality in every corner of the world by the year 2015. The establishment of MDG 6—aimed at halting and reversing the spread of communicable diseases—illustrates the widespread recognition of the toll that communicable diseases are taking and the importance of bringing them under control.[1] While significant

1. Specifically, MDG 6 aims to combat HIV/AIDS, malaria, and other diseases and lays out three general targets: (1) have halted and begun to reverse the spread of HIV/AIDS by 2015; (2) have achieved universal access to treatment for HIV/AIDS for all those who need it by 2010; and (3) have halted and begun to reverse the incidence of malaria and other major diseases by 2015. For more information on the MDGs and progress toward achieving them, see the UN's website: www.un.org/millenniumgoals/.

progress has been made toward achieving MDG 6 in some countries and communities, there is growing concern that others will fall far short of the goal when the 2015 deadline arrives. Many stakeholders are scrambling to come up with new approaches to reaching all of the MDGs, including number 6, realizing that we need to think more creatively about the resources we have to leverage in the drive to achieving them, and sounding the call for "all hands on deck" for the final push and beyond.

The Global Fund to Fight AIDS, Tuberculosis and Malaria (the Global Fund) was established in 2002 as one reflection of the international community's strong commitment to fighting these three major communicable diseases. Since then, it has committed US$19.3 billion—raised from governments, corporations, and private foundations—for programs in 144 countries around the world.[2] However, despite the progress that has been made in the few short years since its founding, there are still approximately 5 million people who become newly infected with HIV and about 3 million who die from AIDS every year. Tuberculosis kills close to 2 million people annually, and malaria causes more than 1 million deaths every year, with 90 percent of its victims in Africa, the vast majority of whom are children under the age of five. While the international response to these diseases is growing, their spread continues to outpace progress made in prevention and treatment, requiring stronger responses from all sectors of society.

There are a number of misperceptions about communicable diseases that have helped fuel the fire and hindered efforts to stem the spread of these diseases.[3] There is still a tendency to think of HIV/AIDS as a disease that affects certain high-risk groups such as men who have sex with men (MSM), commercial sex workers (CSWs), and injecting drug users (IDUs). But as the epidemic has grown, its reach has extended far beyond these more traditional risk groups, spreading throughout the general population. In fact, in some countries married women are now the group at highest risk, infected by their husbands who unknowingly pass it on to them. Women are more likely to be infected with HIV than men in some African countries—as much as five times more at risk in some age groups—and the ratio of female-to-male infection rates are rising in many countries where the epidemic is growing, notably in East

2. Figures for Global Fund operations are current as of June 2010.
3. The following discussion of misperceptions of the three diseases is drawn from remarks by Joelle Tanguy, then managing director of the Global Business Coalition on HIV/AIDS, Tuberculosis and Malaria, at an FGFJ symposium on "Corporate Responses to Communicable Diseases" in Tokyo on February 5, 2007.

Asia. It is critical, therefore, that we recognize that the face of AIDS is changing and acknowledge the implications it has for both prevention and treatment programs.

Similarly, many people identify AIDS as an African disease—and indeed the highest rates of infection are still found in Africa—but some of the fastest-growing infection rates in the world are found in emerging markets, such as China, Russia, and Eastern Europe. Prevalence rates in Asia are still much lower than those in Africa, but the larger population sizes in Asia mean that the sheer number of people infected is alarmingly large in some countries. In 2006, there were an estimated 8.6 million people infected with HIV in Asia—roughly 960,000 of whom became newly infected that year—and more than 600,000 people in Asia died of AIDS in that same year.[4] Ambitious prevention efforts in parts of Asia—most notably Thailand and its 100 Percent Condom Program, aimed at CSWs and their clients—have proven successful in lowering infection rates among certain segments of Asia's population, but rates continue to climb throughout much of the region. Rates have also begun to rise among new risk groups in countries that have successfully slowed the overall spread of new infection. Sticking with the example of Thailand, infection rates have been climbing rapidly among young girls, who were not a target of the 100 Percent Condom Program.[5] Treating the growing number of HIV-infected people in Asia is also becoming a major challenge. The number of people in Asia receiving antiretroviral (ARV) treatment more than tripled between 2003 and 2006, reaching an estimated 235,000 people by the middle of the year. But despite the impressive progress, that number still represents only 16 percent of those believed to need treatment in Asia.[6]

Tuberculosis is often thought of as a disease of the past, but in fact infection rates are rising, and it is reemerging as a deadly threat around the world today. The disease is most dangerous in elderly people or people with suppressed immune systems. In most cases, treatment is effective for young, healthy patients, but treatment regimens require patients to take a combination of pills every day for a long period of time—at least six months—and failure to continue treatment contributes to the emergence of deadly drug-resistant strains. Every continent has

4. UNAIDS and WHO, "2006 Epi Update Fact Sheet Asia" (November 21, 2006), data.unaids.org/pub/EpiReport/2006/20061121_epi_fs_a_en.pdf.
5. Interview with Patrick Brenny, UNAIDS country coordinator of Thailand, November 7, 2005.
6. UNAIDS and WHO, "2006 Epi Update Fact Sheet Asia."

experienced an outbreak of multidrug-resistant tuberculosis in recent years, with some countries experiencing alarming incidences of highly dangerous strains of extreme drug-resistant tuberculosis, sparking fears that tuberculosis could reemerge as a widespread, significant threat even to young, healthy adults.

Malaria is also often considered an African disease. While it is true that the majority of deaths due to malaria occur in Africa, the disease is also widespread and often fatal in Asia. In fact, some of the most drug-resistant strains of malaria can be found in Southeast Asia. As residents of malaria-free areas find themselves travelling to malarial zones more frequently—either for work or pleasure—everyone needs to be aware of the danger of malaria, how to prevent infection, and where to go to receive timely, effective treatment.

There has been a growing recognition that diseases such as HIV/AIDS, tuberculosis, and malaria are not merely public health issues. They are also important economic issues, with dire impacts on economic growth even as they are spurred along by rapid growth and mobility. As goods and people move across national borders with increasing ease, so do communicable diseases. At the same time, as markets become more interdependent, challenges in one country can have dire consequences for markets in neighboring countries and countries halfway around the world alike.

Even those who will never personally become infected with these three diseases are not immune to their impact. The economic, political, and security implications have proven disastrous in countries with high infection rates and particularly in places with high rates of HIV infection, which overwhelmingly strikes people in what should be their most productive years. Loss of productivity due to death, illness, and responsibilities to care for sick family members has already begun to slow economic growth in many African countries. Political debates about treatment and the public sector's responsibility have contributed to political turmoil and further eroded many communities' resilience to other human security challenges. In addition, countries with high HIV infection rates have suffered the loss of military personnel to AIDS, making it increasingly difficult for them to continue to protect their civilian populations.

Estimates of the impact of HIV on a country's gross domestic product (GDP) are difficult to generate, but according to some economists, HIV infection in Africa has likely resulted in close to a 1 percent decrease in GDP growth every year, and some estimate that the number is higher than 2 percent in countries with infection rates higher than 20 percent.[7] Similarly, it is estimated that malaria has resulted in annual economic losses of approximately US$12 billion in Africa and is causing GDP growth to slow by 1.3 percent every year.[8] All three diseases are already having a profound impact not only in sub-Saharan Africa but also on markets around the world. Asia and other emerging markets are also being hit hard, leading companies to realize that they need to take global approaches to dealing with communicable diseases, focusing on the immediate impact on their employees—affecting a company's productivity—as well as on the longer-term impact on their consumer bases.

For example, while Japan is fortunate to have low infection rates within its own borders, the country is dependent on workforces and markets around the world that are more directly affected by the spread of communicable diseases. Because most of Japan's energy and food comes from overseas, disruptions in foreign workforces due to illness will decrease supply and push up prices in Japan. It is important, therefore, that executives and consumers from low-prevalence countries like Japan understand their own reliance on healthy, productive workforces overseas and, by extension, understand why fighting communicable diseases has become their business as well.

This focus on a healthy, productive workforce provides a useful perspective for the evolution of corporate social responsibility in Japan. It is when employers view their employees as important company assets, not charity cases, that fighting the spread and impact of communicable diseases makes clear business sense. When employees need support or care, providing that becomes a business imperative. This is not a new concept for Japanese companies, which have long provided generous healthcare benefits to their workforces.

Helping prevent the spread of disease in the workplace as well as in surrounding communities is one key way for companies to protect their employees. Another important step is providing treatment for those who are already infected and adjusting their workload and responsibilities, if necessary, to accommodate their physical condition. In that way, employers can shift discussions in the workplace on diseases like AIDS

---

7. United States Agency for International Development, "How Does HIV/AIDS Affect African Businesses?" 6.
8. World Bank, "Malaria: Overview of the Booster Program for Malaria Control in the Africa Region" (Updated September 2009), web.worldbank.org/WBSITE/EXTERNAL/NEWS/0,,contentMDK:20912730~pagePK:64257043~piPK:437376~print:Y~theSitePK:4607,00.html.

away from an excessive focus on death and illness and talk more about the individuals who are impacted by the disease so that they can live healthier, more productive lives.

It is important, however, to keep in mind that a person who begins receiving ARV treatment for HIV/AIDS has to continue taking the drugs for the rest of his or her life. The cost per person is high, and given that patients may be able to live for another 40 years with treatment, the potential cost can seem quite daunting for employers. Therefore, it is important that companies analyze the cost of preventing disease compared with that of treating it. Most companies find that the cost of engaging in the fight against communicable diseases—in terms of finances, time, and commitment—is not very significant, but the cost of not doing anything is high. That is obvious if one looks at the countries that have not done anything to address AIDS or where the business response has lagged behind the government response; infection rates in those countries continue to climb.

Insurance companies also need to provide leadership in this area. In countries where health insurance is tied to employment, an HIV-positive person might enjoy sufficient health benefits in one company, but they find that they cannot advance their career by changing companies or even moving overseas because they will no longer be insurable to receive the life-saving treatment upon which they depend.

Japan offers a good example of tuberculosis control based on a clear cost-benefit analysis. More than 50 years ago, companies found that total losses attributed to the disease in terms of lost productivity, the cost of training replacement workers, and so on, exceeded 10 percent of total wages, so they knew that they had to do something to stop its spread and began to do so even before the public sector got involved. Japanese companies started having employees get chest X-rays twice a year to catch and contain cases of active tuberculosis and immediately found that incidences of disease decreased and productivity—of individual companies and of the country as a whole—increased. Because companies were taking strong action to diagnose and prevent the disease early, they were taking some of the burden off of the Ministry of Health, allowing it to focus on other issues and build a strong public health system during the early years after World War II. This allowed companies to expand into dealing with other lifestyle-related diseases, and today the Japanese workforce enjoys high levels of health and welfare.

While these explanations and most of the statistics concerning the economic impact of communicable diseases focus on macro-level effects, the micro-level economic impact can be utterly devastating. Communicable diseases can devastate households, with any one of these infections causing as much as an 80 percent decline in household income.[9] The economic impact is particularly severe in poorer communities that do not have adequate access to treatment or safety nets to compensate for lost productivity of sick family members and their caregivers. AIDS, in particular, most often strikes people in their most productive years, so illness or death due to AIDS often means a family loses its key breadwinner. Family income is also lost when healthy members take time off of work to care for sick members or to attend funerals. UNAIDS estimates that there are more than 25 million children around the world who have been orphaned as a result of AIDS, and many countries in Africa are experiencing an appalling rise in the number of child-headed households as a result.[10]

Why Corporate Engagement?

When the Global Fund was created, the world was already 20 years into the AIDS epidemic, but primary responsibility for fighting AIDS was still seen in many places as lying with the public sector or, more precisely, the public health sector. However, in recent years, multisectoral engagement and cross-sectoral cooperation have grown, and many more corporations have come to view the fight against the spread of HIV/AIDS and other communicable diseases as being in their own interest as well.

The role of governments and political leadership in fighting the spread of communicable diseases cannot be overstated. Many countries where political and governmental leaders responded with denial and accusations regarding the reasons why HIV/AIDS was spreading—and the appropriate responses to dealing with the spread—found that the epidemics in their countries were so far out of their control once they began to acknowledge the need for strong action, that they had become prohibitively costly in terms both of financial resources and of human lives lost. In other countries where strong political commitments were made, such as in Thailand with its 100 Percent Condom Program, there has been a certain level of success in reducing the spread of new infections and in

9. Alan Whiteside, "Poverty and HIV/AIDS in Africa," *Third World Quarterly* 23, no. 2 (2002): 328.
10. UNAIDS, "Children and Orphans," www.unaids.org/en/PolicyAndPractice/KeyPopulations/ChildAndOrphans/.

beginning to treat and care for those who are infected. In short, it is hard to imagine any kind of progress in the fight against AIDS without strong governmental leadership.

Still, the sheer magnitude of the challenge that the world faces as a result of the spread of communicable diseases means that no single sector can be expected to deal with them sufficiently. For example, for Thailand to keep 600,000 HIV-positive people alive with ARV treatment will cost about US$6 billion per year. Today, people with HIV/AIDS can live for as long as 30 years, which means that the total cost of keeping them alive becomes US$180 billion.[11] Governments, particularly in poor countries that are dealing with many other challenges to the daily survival of their citizens, do not have these kinds of resources. Without support from other sectors, there is no chance that governments alone can win the fight against communicable diseases.

In addition, communicable diseases by nature are closely intertwined with other threats faced by individuals and communities around the world, including poverty, migration, inequality, environmental degradation, and lack of access to education, sustainable food sources, and clean water. As such, they must be addressed in a comprehensive manner that addresses these interlinkages. In other words, a human security approach that includes cross-sectoral partnership and multidisciplinary cooperation to build resilience is essential.

In addition to a recognition of the importance of healthy, happy, and productive employees, many corporations around the world that are actively engaged in the fight against communicable diseases have gotten involved because, as beneficiaries of globalization, they feel a responsibility to help alleviate some of the negative impact of this trend. By helping support the communities in which they operate, these corporations are able to build good will and gain the respect and appreciation of their employees and potential customers and clients, which in turn helps their own bottom line.

On the other hand, there has been more research in recent years on the impact that certain working conditions have on increasing employees' vulnerability to disease. It should be noted that this increased vulnerability is not an inevitable consequence of corporate activities. Corporations have proven that even modest efforts to anticipate potential negative impacts and to proactively address the problem can have significant

11. Comments by Anthony Pramualratana, executive director of the Thailand Business Coalition on AIDS, at an FGFJ symposium on "Corporate Responses to Communicable Diseases" in Tokyo on February 5, 2007.

positive impacts on both the health of their employees and the health of their companies.

For example, large construction projects generally employ young males on a temporary basis, and it is not uncommon for employees to temporarily relocate domestically or internationally for the duration of the projects they are working on. This temporary relocation can put them at risk of HIV infection as they are more likely to engage in commercial sex or drug use to help them deal with the stress and isolation of being away from their families and communities and as they find themselves with some extra spending money. Too often, when they return to their home communities or move on to the next job site, they unknowingly take an HIV infection with them. Clear evidence of this phenomenon has prompted some construction companies and their financiers to incorporate HIV prevention measures into their workplans, such as Taisei Construction did for a large bridge construction project it undertook in Vietnam with financing from the Japan Bank for International Cooperation (JBIC).

In the case of tuberculosis, close quarters in factories place employees at risk of contracting this airborne disease from coworkers. It is, therefore, clearly in the interests of factory owners to control tuberculosis transmission on factory floors and in the communities where their employees live by encouraging testing, assuring employees that they will not lose their jobs if they test positive, and providing treatment so that they can return to work as quickly as possible. Central Azucarera Don Pedro (CADPI), a major Filipino sugar manufacturer, has been engaged in these kinds of activities in the Philippines, where tuberculosis rates are still relatively high.

Malaria often becomes a particular problem for companies in the extraction business. The nature of the industry requires that worksites be established where the relevant natural resources are found, and that often means they are located in malarial zones. Employees who work outdoors in areas where malaria is prevalent risk infection via mosquito bites while they are working, but they are also at risk of infection where they live, often in employee compounds near their worksites. In addition to the impact on individual families, lost productivity due to malaria-related illness has the potential to slow projects down, which increases the cost of the project. Companies like ExxonMobil have found that it is more cost-effective for them to try to protect their employees from malaria infection than to try to deal with the lost productivity due to illness.

Given this context, it has become clear that the corporate sector has an important role to play in the fight against communicable diseases. Not only is the sector experiencing serious impacts as a result of the spread of disease, but it also has the resources to significantly complement contributions from the public and civil society sectors. Corporations can educate their employees about prevention and stigma, often reaching people who would not be reached by programs implemented by other sectors, simply because they have the authority to require their employees to attend training sessions during working hours. Most corporations are also skilled at public relations and advertising, so they can reach large segments of the population outside of their workforces with compelling messages about prevention and stigma.

Standard Chartered Bank offers a good example of a company that reaches out to its employees through workplace programs and offers prevention education programs upon request to its clients and host communities. M·A·C Cosmetics reaches out to the general public through large-scale awareness-raising campaigns with celebrity spokesmodels, and MTV airs public service announcements and develops other programs to reach out to young viewers. Bayer China uses its core competency in communications to help educate media professionals on HIV prevention and stigma so that they can explain the epidemic in a balanced fashion to a wide audience.

Companies also have financial resources and business skills that can be applied to prevention and treatment campaigns. Most of the companies profiled in this volume—and many others that are not included in this study—make direct financial contributions to organizations dealing with communicable diseases. Chevron, for example, is the largest corporate donor to the Global Fund, having committed US$25 million to its Corporate Champions Program. ExxonMobil has become a major funder in the campaign against malaria, supporting efforts aimed at eradicating malaria and mitigating its effects. M·A·C Cosmetics has set up the M·A·C AIDS Fund to support grassroots service provision and advocacy initiatives, financed entirely by revenue from a dedicated line of lipstick and lip gloss.

In countries with low levels of infrastructure development, the supply and distribution networks that companies have developed can play a vital role in getting information and life-saving medications to hard-to-reach populations. Coca-Cola, for example, arranges for distributors carrying its beverages to rural areas to also carry prevention education materials for NGOs. While this does not add anything to the company's transportation costs, it provides an invaluable service to organizations that otherwise would not be able to reach these remote locations.

Companies have also found that the products and services that they sell can be used in the fight against communicable diseases. Sumitomo Chemical, for example, was already making insecticides when it discovered that it could also create a new kind of longer-lasting bed net, which has proven to be one of the most effective tools for preventing malaria transmission in developing countries. It has since started to transfer that technology to countries with high malaria disease burdens so that they can produce more nets than could be produced in Sumitomo Chemical's existing facilities and help boost the local economy at the same time.

Finally, corporate leaders have a unique role to play as respected members of their communities. One of the biggest barriers to fighting the spread of AIDS and tuberculosis has been the stigma associated with these diseases and the fear of isolation or loss of employment. This prevents them from getting the treatment they need and from taking necessary steps to avoid spreading their infections to others. But, when corporate leaders make a public show of solidarity with those affected by these diseases, as the CEO of Levi Strauss did when he decided to personally hand out pamphlets on AIDS early in the epidemic, they send a strong message that AIDS is something that can be talked about openly and civilly in the workplace. Similarly, when CEOs of several Standard Chartered Bank branches publicly announced that they had taken HIV tests, they set an important example for their employees and peers that no one should consider themselves exempt from risk.

How Companies Get Involved

Every company has its own unique reasons for getting involved in the fight against communicable diseases and its own unique process for making that decision, but one theme that was repeated in every interview for this project was the vital role of leadership. In most of the cases, either the top leadership of the company or top leaders in an overseas branch recognized the threat posed by communicable diseases and decided to take bold action. In cases where it was company medical personnel who first recognized the importance of corporate engagement, such as in the case of Anglo American, their first task was convincing their bosses not only to allow their companies to get engaged but to take ownership of the process and make engagement in the fight against communicable diseases a core value of the entire company.

In some cases, the initiative came from overseas branches in hard-hit areas where managers found they had no choice but to deal proactively with communicable diseases because of the impact on their workforces. Companies were losing employees and experiencing high levels of absenteeism as sick employees stayed home and others had to miss work either to take care of sick family members or to attend funerals. They found they simply could not operate without a healthy workforce. Toyota and DaimlerChrysler are two companies that followed this model, driven by the impact of high infection rates in their plants in South Africa.

In other cases, companies chose to engage in the fight against communicable diseases because they found, particularly in the AIDS epidemic, that the target populations for their products and services were the same populations that were being hit hard by the epidemic. AIDS quickly became a very personal issue for these companies, but it also became a business imperative, as they needed to find a way to protect those people who constituted their market. This was the case for M·A·C Cosmetics and MTV, both of which got involved early in the United States, where the creative communities were initially among the most vulnerable to infection. MTV has been particularly well placed to raise awareness because of its ability to speak to young people, who are at high risk of infection but who are also difficult for other stakeholders to reach.

For some companies that did not have as visible a stake in the fight against communicable diseases, firm decisions by their CEOs and other top executives led to bold public engagement. Levi Strauss and Standard Chartered Bank are two such examples. While no company is immune to the effects of communicable diseases, neither of these companies were plagued with the devastating economic effects experienced by companies whose workforces or markets comprised the most vulnerable populations. Still, they quickly recognized the broader societal impact of AIDS in their communities and their own leadership potential in this area.

For other companies, interest grew out of work they were already doing that eventually led them to become engaged. For example, when Sumitomo Chemical began developing its long-lasting insecticide nets, its aim was to expand its existing technology into new products that it could market, not to become a major player in protecting people from malaria. It was only when it began to see that added benefit of joining this global fight that it combined its expertise in chemicals with a focus specifically on preventing malaria transmission. Similarly, APCO, a global public affairs and communications company, had never been involved in work related to HIV or other sexually transmitted infections until it was commissioned to do a marketing study on condoms, which opened employees' eyes to the important role that condoms can play in protecting people from a range of dangerous infections.

Companies cannot survive unless they are able to sell their products and services to people. This requires providing quality goods and services that fulfill some kind of need or desire in people's lives, but it also requires having a name that people recognize and respect. None of the companies in this study got involved in the fight against communicable diseases simply as a means of improving their public image, but they all found that their activities are good for their corporate reputation and help them stand out among their competitors rather than hurting their image. In addition, most of the company representatives who were interviewed for the project explained that the attention they have received has helped make them more attractive not only to consumers but to prospective employees as well.

Many of the companies included in this project got involved partly as a way to give back to the communities where they operate, particularly those with large overseas operations. ExxonMobil, for example, found it important to expand its programs beyond its own employees and their families. This is in part because malaria—like other communicable diseases—does not discriminate, putting employees at risk when the incidence in their communities is high. It is also because the good will that they develop as a result of their community involvement makes it easier for them to carry out their business activities, often in ways that are impossible to quantify. In the case of Standard Chartered Bank, which already provides valuable financial services in communities around the world, profits are ultimately sent back to the UK, but the non-monetary investments that the company makes in its host communities through its training and awareness-raising activities help make it a more welcome presence. For Taisei's bridge construction project in Vietnam, it was the public-sector financing agency, JBIC, that urged the company to include an HIV-prevention component in its business plan in response to concerns that other JBIC-supported projects might have unwittingly contributed to the spread of HIV infection in other project locations.

While it is not uncommon for an initiative to begin in an overseas office where the impact of disease has been more widespread and severe, that experience still needs to be taken back to headquarters so that top executives there are aware of the urgency of the problem and can begin to institutionalize a response throughout the company—not just in one or two branches—so that engagement in the fight against communicable diseases becomes a part of the company's culture. This can be a difficult task, particularly when executives in corporate headquarters have largely been shielded from witnessing firsthand the devastating effects of communicable diseases and, importantly, the positive business impact of even modest investments in the fight against them. International companies like DaimlerChrylser and Standard Chartered Bank eventually translated their experience fighting AIDS in certain overseas branches into company-wide policy, developing workplace programs and training curricula that apply to their employees around the world. Others, including Toyota and Taisei, are at earlier stages in their efforts to institutionalize their engagement in the fight against AIDS at headquarters, and more will need to be done to expose top decision makers to the threats their companies face and to their potential as corporations to reduce risk.

Types of Involvement

The companies profiled in this study have all taken their own unique approaches to dealing with the challenges of communicable diseases in their workplaces, their markets, and their communities. As pioneers, they have had to carve out their own paths, and as diverse companies they have had to find solutions that are appropriate to their own sectors, needs, resources, abilities, and cultures.

That said, their initiatives can be broadly categorized into six types of activities, discussed below. Most of the companies have engaged in one or more of these activities, either simultaneously or at different periods in time. This is by no means an exhaustive list of the types of activities that companies around the world engage in to fight the spread and impact of communicable diseases, and in the future companies will no doubt come up with new, innovative approaches that have yet to be witnessed.

Workplace policy

One of the first steps many of the companies took when they recognized the toll that communicable diseases were taking on their employees was to develop explicit workplace policies to articulate top management's expectations for how the diseases should be viewed and dealt with in the workplace. Recognizing first and foremost that all employees should be treated as human beings, regardless of their health status, most HIV/AIDS and tuberculosis workplace policies begin with statements of nondiscrimination against employees who are infected or suspected to be infected. HIV/AIDS workplace policies generally denounce mandatory testing but strongly encourage voluntary testing as a way for employees to both know their own risk of spreading infection to others and receive timely treatment if they test positive, increasing their chances of remaining healthy and productive for a longer period of time. Policies also put in place systems for ensuring that test results are kept confidential unless an employee chooses to disclose his or her infection status.

CADPI's workplace policy on tuberculosis assures employees that they will be able to return to work as soon as it can be confirmed that they are no longer contagious, provided they continue taking their prescribed drug regimen. In the case of malaria, though, which does not carry the same stigma as AIDS and tuberculosis, ExxonMobil's workplace policy requires all non-immune staff in malaria-endemic areas to take prophylaxis against infection and mandates that any employee who exhibits symptoms of malaria get tested so that he or she can begin treatment immediately if infected, which has been proven to reduce malaria's severity and the likelihood that it will be fatal.

Workplace prevention and treatment programs

In addition to these policies, many of the profiled companies have developed workplace programs aimed at preventing infection in their employees and keeping those who are infected alive, healthy, and productive for as long as possible. Recognizing the high cost of treating employees with HIV/AIDS, many of the programs emphasize activities aimed at preventing new infections. Some companies incorporate sessions on the prevention of HIV/AIDS, tuberculosis, or malaria into their training programs for new employees, who tend to be large, captive audiences. They also provide ongoing prevention education to current employees through regular training sessions, awareness-raising events, and forums for confidential inquiries.

Reducing stigma and discrimination surrounding HIV/AIDS and tuberculosis does not only protect the rights of infected employees; it also helps prevent further spread by making people feel more comfortable with testing because it increases their confidence that they will be treated the same by their colleagues regardless of the test results. Therefore, prevention education activities inside companies generally include strong components aimed at reducing stigma and discrimination. One method that some companies have found effective has been the inclusion of

HIV-positive trainers in educational sessions so that their employees can see that people living with HIV are people, just like they are.

As mentioned above, early detection of HIV, tuberculosis, and malaria helps decrease the chances that infection will be passed on to others and improves the prognosis of those who are infected if they commit to timely and appropriate treatment. Workplace programs therefore also focus on encouraging testing. In the case of malaria and tuberculosis, the emphasis is on teaching people how to recognize symptoms, where they can go to get tested, and what can be done if they test positive. In the case of HIV, the emphasis is on encouraging everyone to get tested even in the absence of any symptoms. Some companies provide testing facilities within the workplace, making it easy for employees to get tested. These companies have had to carefully craft their programs to assure employees that the results of their test will be kept confidential. Many companies also help their employees get tested off-site in order to further assure confidentiality. DaimlerChrysler even goes so far as to provide financial incentives to local clinics in South Africa to offer testing services to its employees, their families, and others in the community.

People with HIV can live healthy, productive lives for decades after infection, thanks to the emergence and availability of ARV drugs. However, companies have had to recognize that employees living with HIV/AIDS are still likely to face health challenges from their infection as well as from the drugs' side effects. Therefore, instead of terminating employees who are no longer physically able to carry out their assigned duties, some companies have developed programs for reassigning tasks for HIV-positive employees—as needed and as deemed reasonable—in the same way that they make accommodations for employees facing any other health challenge.

Finally, despite the high cost of providing ARV treatment, many companies have found that it still makes more sense—from a business as well as moral standpoint—to ensure that their employees are treated than to lose them due to health-related reasons. Some companies with on-site medical facilities offer treatment in the workplace, although they have had to take precautions to assure confidentiality. Others contract with outside clinics and insurance schemes to make sure that ARV and other treatments are available to all their employees who need them.

Core competencies

Core competencies refers to those things that a company does best. A company's core competencies include the obvious things, such as the product or service that it sells, as well as the less obvious things, such as the skills that its employees have developed in order to produce a product or perform a service and the structures that it has put in place to conduct its business effectively. Several of the companies included in this study have lent their own core competencies to the fight against communicable diseases.

Sumitomo Chemical is a good example of a company that has chosen to leverage one of its products—insecticides—in the fight against malaria. By weaving the insecticide into the bednets that it produces, Sumitomo Chemical was able to produce a revolutionary tool for preventing malaria-spreading mosquito bites in endemic areas. MTV's primary audience as a company is youth aged 13 to 25, and it has leveraged its ability to reach out to this demographic around the world to raise awareness of the risk of HIV infection, encourage safe behavior, and break down the stigma and discrimination associated with infection.

Other companies have leveraged core competencies that are less obvious. Bayer China, for example, develops and produces pharmaceuticals, but it has found that it has a different asset that is invaluable in preventing HIV infection: its ability to reach out to the general public to assess needs, market products, and provide health-related information. Recognizing the key role of the media in educating the general public about HIV prevention and in eradicating stigma, Bayer China has developed a program in partnership with a local university to provide training to journalists with an interest in health-related issues. Standard Chartered Bank leveraged its vast network of corporate clients to offer training-of-trainer sessions on HIV/AIDS to representatives of client companies so that they could in turn provide training in their own workplaces. Coca-Cola and its corporate partners bring beverages into some of the most remote communities around the world, and they have leveraged that distribution capacity to deliver condoms and educational materials in areas far beyond where others can reach.

Extension of programs and policies

For the most part, the diseases in question are not spread in the workplace during working hours or as a direct result of particular business activities of the companies examined in these studies. Instead, they are generally spread in the communities where employees live, which is only sometimes directly determined—notably in the case of construction projects and extraction industries—by the nature of the work. Therefore, if employers want to protect their own employees from infection, they cannot ignore the people with whom their employees live and interact on a daily basis. This realization led some of the companies to expand the programs they had developed for their own employees to also cover the communities where their employees live. In the case of Taisei, for example, this meant providing condoms and HIV prevention training to neighboring women working in the commercial sex industry. In the case of CADPI, DaimlerChrysler, and Anglo American, it meant ensuring that people living in communities surrounding their workplaces had the same access to prevention and treatment services that their employees had. Coca-Cola is a unique case because most of its product is assembled and sold by bottling companies in the "Coca-Cola system" that are independent companies. The company decided to expand its program to provide HIV prevention education and ARV treatment to the employees and dependents of all 40 licensed bottlers in its African network.

Volunteerism and philanthropy

In addition to expanding their programs to the surrounding communities, most of the companies are also engaged in more traditional methods of supporting their surrounding communities. Some companies offer incentives to their employees to volunteer their time for various causes, including stemming the spread and impact of communicable diseases. Standard Chartered Bank has a company-wide policy of allowing every employee to take two additional days off per year to do volunteer work related to blindness or HIV/AIDS, the two social issues on which the company places priority. Many of the bank's employees in Thailand have chosen to use that time to conduct HIV training sessions and testing campaigns in nearby communities. Levi Strauss has institutionalized its commitment to volunteerism through its Community Involvement Teams, which are encouraged to volunteer with organizations in their communities, and all of the apparel company's employees in the United States are given five hours of paid leave every month to perform volunteer activities.

Other companies have chosen to form partnerships with local NGOs that provide services for their communities. Not all of the companies have the necessary ties to reach out to the vulnerable populations in the communities where they operate, and few of them actually have the in-house expertise to provide training and services even if they do have appropriate ties. These companies have come to depend heavily on NGOs, which do have both strong connections to communities—particularly high-risk populations—and relevant expertise to implement programs outside of the company's walls.

Finally, many of the companies provide more traditional philanthropy by making grants to organizations active in the fight against communicable diseases. Some have set up grant-making foundations to support local NGOs and other organizations. Coca-Cola's foundation in Africa also provides funding to the company's bottling partners so that they can establish their own programs to provide training and ARV treatment to their employees. M·A·C Cosmetics has developed a unique program whereby the entire selling price of one of its lines of lipstick and lip gloss is donated to organizations through the M·A·C AIDS Fund.

Leadership by example

Corporate executives often find that people look up to them for guidance, both professionally and personally. Employees who want to move up in their companies and industries look to their bosses for hints as to what kind of efforts and behavior are valued and rewarded. Executives in other firms look to the leaders of successful corporations to learn lessons for improving their own business practices. Others in their communities often see successful businessmen and women as natural leaders outside of the workplace. It is no surprise, then, that everyone interviewed for this project talked about the crucial role of leadership in getting and keeping their companies engaged in the fight against communicable diseases.

In many cases, having the top executives talk comfortably about communicable diseases has helped reduce stigma, particularly in the case of HIV/AIDS, setting an example for other employees that not only is it a subject that can be discussed openly, but it is important enough to warrant the time and attention of busy executives. For companies that rely on volunteer peer educators to implement programs in their workplaces and communities, recognition and encouragement from their bosses have proven helpful in motivating employees to take on these additional duties, which lie outside of their formal job descriptions. In addition, executives from some companies decided to publicly get tested for HIV, demonstrating to their employees and others in the community that HIV is a threat to everyone—not just certain marginalized populations—and that getting tested is an important step in combating its spread.

That leadership role does not stop in the workplace. Corporate leaders have also been important advocates for strong commitments to fighting the spread and impact of communicable diseases well beyond the confines of their own companies. Many of them leverage their own experiences to encourage others to engage as well, talking about the benefits their companies have realized as a result of their active engagement. The Global Business Coalition on HIV/AIDS, Tuberculosis and Malaria offers one major platform for leaders of companies active in the fight to reach out to their peers in the business community, and top executives in some of the companies profiled in this volume have been very prominent within that network. Some business leaders are frequently invited to speak about their own experiences in other forums, and they have found that by speaking out they can help influence not only other companies but also policy regarding communicable diseases in the countries where they operate.

Business Impact

While many people agree that helping fight the spread of communicable diseases and mitigate their effects on people around the world is the right thing to do, it is important to remember that corporations have a responsibility to their shareholders and other stakeholders. Therefore, it is only natural that they need to make a strong business case for why their engagement first and foremost helps to further the goals of the corporation. The cases examined in this study offer no shortage of explanations of the business case, some more visible and quantifiable than others.

For companies that depend on large workforces in areas with high infection rates, it quickly became clear that something had to be done about the rising rates of HIV/AIDS, tuberculosis, and malaria that were eroding their workforces. Companies that have implemented strong workplace programs have found that the programs save them money in the long run because they help to reduce absenteeism and employee turnover, both of which have direct effects on a company's productivity and training costs.[12] Some of the companies have also found that associating their brand with the fight against communicable diseases has gained them a larger and more loyal consumer base, as customers increasingly take the impact of

12. See, for example, Frank G. Feeley III, Sydney Rosen, and Patrick J. Connelly, "The Private Sector and HIV/AIDS in Africa: Recent Developments and Implications for Policy," in *The Changing HIV/AIDS Landscape: Selected Papers for the World Bank's Agenda for Action in Africa, 2007–2011*, ed. Elizabeth L. Lule, Richard M. Siefman, and Antonio C. David (Washington DC: International Bank for Reconstruction and Development/World Bank, 2009).

their choices as consumers—both positive and negative—into account as they choose how and where to spend their money.

Companies also cited rewards that are harder to quantify in terms of their impact on the company's bottom line, and many of them were unintended consequences of their programs. High employee morale was one such reward, with Standard Chartered Bank and M·A·C Cosmetics discovering that their HIV/AIDS programs were among the top reasons why young people were attracted to the company to begin with and a reason why they were proud to continue working there. Strong commitment to the fight against communicable diseases has also been an important asset for companies in their relationships with the communities where they operate, particularly those in industries that face criticism and accusations of only taking away from these communities without giving anything back.

Partnership

While there is growing recognition of the important role of corporations in fighting the spread and impact of communicable diseases, as described throughout this volume, it also needs to be noted that corporations are not a "silver bullet" in that fight.[13] No single sector can deal with challenges of the magnitude of communicable diseases on its own, and it is only by accepting that lesson and applying it to the way the different sectors interact that any sustainable progress can be made in the fight against communicable diseases.

The public sector is still the largest actor in the fight in much of the world, but it has become clear that governments do not have sufficient resources to tackle the problems alone. Even if they did have unlimited financial resources, though, they would still need the help of other sectors. While part of any government's role is to provide valuable services to the people living within their borders, people working in the public sector are still often far removed from the communities they serve. Government employees often do not have the daily interaction with their constituencies that corporations do, and they often find some of the most vulnerable populations—CSWs and MSM—difficult to reach because of legal issues, social and political taboos against discussions about sex, as

13. This point was reinforced in the third Global Compact Leaders Summit in June 2010. See United Nations Global Compact Office, *Coming of Age: UN-Private Sector Collaboration Since 2000* (New York: UN Global Compact, 2010), 6.

well as a lack of trust. Corporations make important contributions to the fight, but they are still limited in what they can do because they have a responsibility to their shareholders and cannot undertake activities that they know will be bad for business. While NGOs have access to some of the key populations in the fight, possess technical expertise in the field, and often enjoy more flexibility and autonomy, they generally lack the financial and human resources needed to fight communicable diseases on their own.

Partnership, therefore, is a key to winning the battle against communicable diseases, and all of the cases presented in this volume include some type of partnership developed to meet program goals. In each, partnerships have been successful to some degree because the parties share a common overriding goal and understand the important strengths that each brings to the table.

In countries with weak infrastructure, companies were already developing on their own the infrastructure that they needed to carry out their business activities long before they became engaged in the fight against communicable diseases. This has proven to be a valuable asset as they have expanded their activities to engage in the fight. For example, Coca-Cola partners with NGOs in hard-to-reach areas to distribute condoms and educational materials on HIV/AIDS using the company's delivery network throughout Africa. Similarly, corporations in the Philippines lend their logistics management skills and their distribution systems to local health centers to help distrubute drugs for tuberculosis treatment that require the same careful temperature-controlled transportation that some food and beverages do. In Tanzania, Unilever Tea agreed to provide non-employees in one community where it operates with access to its company clinic in exchange for government provision of ARV drugs to both employees and non-employees using the clinic.

Corporations also offer an ideal venue for training and awareness-raising programs since they generally have a more captive audience than governments or NGOs. While actors in the public sector and civil society cannot require that people take part in training programs, corporations routinely offer mandatory training sessions to their employees in order to boost performance. By integrating modules on communicable diseases into such training sessions, they are able to reach large segments of the population who might not have chosen to attend a training session if it were held by government agencies or NGOs. Corporations, on the other hand, routinely offer mandatory training sessions to their employees in order to boost performance, and by integrating modules on communicable diseases, they are able to reach large segments of the population who might not have otherwise chosen to attend training sessions by government agencies or NGOs.

In countries that already have established national programs for dealing with communicable diseases, companies might take on the role of informing their employees about those services and helping them gain access, but they depend on the public sector to actually provide the services. Helping their employees use these government services not only saves companies the expense of having to provide their own testing and treatment services; employees are also often more comfortable accessing services outside of their workplaces where they feel more confident that their serostatus will not be revealed to their coworkers, an important precaution considering that the stigma and discrimination against people with HIV is a major impediment in the campaign to convince people to get tested and seek treatment if necessary.

Corporations in many industries, as well as many government agencies, lack the technical expertise needed to provide services accurately and effectively, and it is in these cases that NGOs play a crucial role in project implementation. As mentioned above, NGOs can also often reach vulnerable populations, including those working in the informal sector, more effectively. In addition, NGOs have successfully brought people who are infected or affected by a communicable disease into their training programs to talk openly about their own experiences as a way to expose trainees to the day-to-day realities these people face, as well as to break down some of the stigma by putting a human face on the diseases.

Finally, while none of the companies in this study cited positive publicity as their primary reason for engaging in the fight against communicable diseases, most have found that positive attention is an important by-product of their efforts. Partnership with NGOs and government agencies often helps bring attention to the work they are doing, making it known well beyond the company walls.

Despite these strong reasons for each sector to work in partnership rather than on their own, partnerships are not always easy to form, and a number of factors need to be taken into consideration. First, there needs to be a clear understanding of why it is in each sector's interests to be engaged. There is most likely an overall shared goal of saving lives in their communities and preventing the threat of communicable diseases from growing further, and that goal needs to be articulated and confirmed by all parties. But there also needs to be an acknowledgement that each party has other objectives, all of which are important and need to be respected by the other parties, even if they do not necessarily share those objectives. Each party also has different ways of defining and measuring success, and it is helpful if they all understand what this is for the others from the outset so that determinations of success are less likely to be challenged down the road. Second, there needs to be a common understanding of each party's relative strengths and weaknesses and an appreciation for the strengths that each party brings to the table. This helps address the third consideration, which is a clear division of labor. Corporations, governments, and NGOs have different approaches to how they operate, and those approaches are more likely to come into conflict in the absence of a clear division of labor established in the planning stage of the partnership.

Challenges

The cases presented in this volume were chosen because they are among some of the most successful examples of corporate engagement in the fight against communicable diseases from around the world. Still, they have not been immune to the many challenges that corporations face in their engagement.

One of the first challenges that corporations face is gaining a clear understanding of communicable diseases, partly because of the misperceptions outlined above. In the case of HIV/AIDS, it is still common for employers to think that if their employees do not fit into one or more of the traditional high-risk populations—CSWs, MSM, IDUs—then they are not really at risk. Similarly, since infection rates are highest in Africa, people tend to think that they do not face any particular risk if they reside outside of the continent. Since people infected with HIV do not exhibit any outward symptoms for years after infection, employers have few mechanisms for understanding how many of their employees are infected or at risk. On top of that, there is still a lack of good data on the impact that communicable diseases have on any individual business.

A second challenge companies have faced deals with the scope and endurance of communicable diseases. Particularly in the case of AIDS, treatment requires a sustained commitment and significant financial resources for decades to come in order to provide treatment to everyone who needs it and will need it in the future. For many corporations this reality makes provision of ARV to employees—let alone their families and others in the surrounding community—too overwhelming to even begin. This is a challenge that is not unique to corporations. With other competing challenges around the world, it is difficult to maintain the interest that has been built in fighting communicable diseases. As treatment becomes more easily available, people lose their sense of urgency and tire of hearing about prevention, a complacency that leads to resurgence of risky behavior.

At the political level, it is already proving difficult to keep communicable diseases prominently on the global policy agenda, so it is only natural that it would be equally challenging to keep it high on any one company's agenda. As new leadership comes into a company, they often want to make their own mark by making a commitment to a new field rather than just continuing the work of their predecessor. Furthermore, during economic downturns, companies that lose profits have to cut costs, and it becomes more difficult to justify preserving programs that are not explicitly aimed at generating revenue. Some companies have tried to address this challenge by institutionalizing their efforts aimed at fighting communicable diseases in order to shield them from these trends. For example, MTV assembled a small team within the company that is dedicated solely to working on AIDS-related programming, ensuring that members of that team do not get sidetracked by other emerging duties. Other companies set up foundations with explicit mandates to contribute to the fight against communicable diseases in order to give more sustainability to their efforts.

Third, as discussed above, companies found that they could not effectively address communicable diseases among their employees if they limit their programs to people inside the company. While employers have some control over how their employees behave in the workplace, they cannot control what they do on their own time. Further, they could make training for employees compulsory, but they could not do the same for others in the community. Therefore, they have had to find new, creative ways to reach out to the community, and this is one area in which NGOs have become invaluable partners for some of the corporations.

Fourth, also discussed above, there was not always agreement between headquarters and overseas branches about the need to invest in the fight against communicable diseases. For managers working in branches in hard-hit countries, it was impossible to ignore the toll that communicable diseases were taking on employees and markets, so it was relatively easy to understand the need for engagement. But, for those who have never witnessed the devastation firsthand, it is more difficult to comprehend the impact of communicable diseases on a company's productivity and, therefore, difficult to understand the business case for investment in the fight against the diseases. Without a company-wide commitment to communicable diseases, it is difficult to take lessons learned in an overseas branch in one hard-hit country to another overseas branch of the same company in a country at risk of being hit hard in the future.

Fifth, stigma associated with HIV/AIDS and tuberculosis and taboos against talking about some of the behaviors that result in HIV transmission—sex and drug use—can make it difficult to convince people of the appropriateness for corporations to deal with communicable diseases. Since it is often behaviors outside of the workplace that lead to infection, it is not always easy for corporate executives to convince their colleagues that it is still the company's business to keep their employees and markets healthy. Better forecasting on the potential negative impact of communicable diseases, as well as more data on the actual business impact that these kinds of programs have on a company's bottom line might provide executives with strong rationales and help them overcome this hurdle more easily.

This leads to the final challenge: measuring impact and evaluating performance. Evaluation is an important tool for companies to use in determining the value and appropriateness of what they are doing. Progress on communicable diseases, however, is difficult to measure and assign value to. Measuring the impact of prevention requires looking at what did not happen rather than what did happen, and it often depends on estimates of what would happen without an intervention as reference points rather than actual events.

◆◆◆

This volume offers a glimpse of 12 companies that have taken bold initiatives to address one of the most significant current global challenges. They are by no means the only companies that have made significant commitments; rather, they were chosen for their diversity of experience, location, culture, and industry. These and other companies have become engaged despite the major challenges discussed here, and by testing out new ways to overcome the challenges, they have helped open new paths that allow other companies to engage as well. They have taken on the fight against communicable diseases both because it is good for business and because they see it simply as the right thing to do. They recognized that they, as corporations and as people within those corporations, have the vast resources, skills, expertise, access, and drive to make a contribution, no matter how big or small. Despite the progress that has been made over the past decade in the fight against the three major communicable diseases, HIV/AIDS, tuberculosis, and malaria all still pose serious threats around the world and have the potential to become significantly worse before they get better. Meanwhile, new communicable diseases continue to emerge, reminding us that this is a long-term battle that we are only beginning to understand. This problem is not going away, but creativity and dedication around the world are critical to our efforts to mitigate the effects of communicable diseases, and everyone has a role to play in those efforts.

Anglo American
Mining for Health

Anglo American is one of the world's leading mining companies. It was founded by Sir Ernest Oppenheimer in 1917 in South Africa under the name of Anglo American South Africa. The company's name derives from its principal sources of funding: the United Kingdom and the United States. At the outset, Anglo American conducted all of its operations in sub-Saharan Africa, mainly in South Africa, but the company expanded its scope of operations thereafter to North America, South America, and Australia. Today, there are six group companies operating in 45 countries, including India and China.[1] The company employs a total of 177,000 people worldwide, most of whom—approximately 120,000—are employed in eastern and southern Africa.

Sub-Saharan Africa has been hit hard by the AIDS pandemic, and HIV infection rates among employees in this region were reported to be 19 percent in 2007.[2] Since the first detection of HIV infection of an employee in 1986, Anglo American has implemented comprehensive countermeasures against AIDS, providing prevention education and AIDS awareness efforts in the workplace and treatment and support for those living with AIDS. In 2002, the company introduced antiretroviral (ARV) treatment for its employees, mainly in the mining areas of South Africa, and it now operates the largest corporate-sector HIV/AIDS program in the world.

Types of activities related to HIV/AIDS

- HIV/AIDS prevention education programs for employees and local residents through the use of peer educators

1. Group companies affiliated with Anglo American include Anglo Platinum, De Beers, Anglo Coal, Anglo Base Metals, Anglo Industrial Minerals, and Anglo Ferrous Metals.
2. Anglo American, *Report to Society 2007* (London: Anglo American, 2008), 33.

- Distribution of free condoms within the company and in host communities
- Promotion of anonymous voluntary counseling and testing (VCT)
- Provision of ARV treatment for HIV-infected employees and their families as part of the company's health program
- Support for AIDS-related activities through the Anglo American Chairman's Fund
- Funding for HIV/AIDS and tuberculosis research

Business Impact of HIV/AIDS

The number of adults infected with HIV in South Africa was estimated to be 5.7 million in 2007, giving it the distinction of being the country with the largest population of HIV-positive people in the world. On top of that, mining is the one of the industries hardest hit by HIV/AIDS. Mining companies have to go where there are natural resources, so they have no control over where they establish their operations. Most employees in mines are seasonal workers who are separated from their families for long periods of times, making them more likely to engage in sex with multiple partners, sometimes including commercial sex workers. Therefore, mining companies must assume that their employees are at high risk for HIV infection. At the same time, due to the arduous physical demands of their work, poor employee health directly impacts their productivity. For these reasons, the AIDS pandemic in sub-Saharan Africa has dealt a direct blow to Anglo American operations. One employee mentioned that he attended about one funeral a week for AIDS victims when he began working for Anglo American in the late 1990s, but that the number had increased to four or five a week by 2001.[3] According to some reports, companies have to train three staff members for every position to compensate for the likelihood of absenteeism due to AIDS-related illness or for the loss of employees from AIDS-related death.

Over a three-year period beginning in 2003, Aurum Health Research—Anglo American's research institute—and the London School of Hygiene and Tropical Medicine undertook a survey of the economic impact of AIDS on Anglo American operations, supported by a grant from GlaxoSmithKline. The study found that if no ARV treatment was provided, the cost of AIDS would amount to 2 percent of all wages, reaching a peak

3. CNN.com, "AIDS: 20 Years of an Epidemic—In South Africa, AIDS Sparks Fear of Devastation," 2003, www.cnn.com (accessed January 15, 2007).

between 2007 and 2009.[4] In 2007, according to an Anglo American health economics study, HIV programs in South Africa cost approximately US$10 million a year. However, the study also showed that costs of providing treatment were beginning to pay for themselves through reduced absenteeism, lower treatment costs for other infections, and fewer lost skills. Now, 95 percent of those on treatment are able to work normally, allowing them to contribute to the economy and continue supporting their families.[5]

Three Zeros

In 2002, Anglo American defined its HIV/AIDS program, which balances prevention, care, support, and treatment, as a "Three Zeros Policy."[6] Under the policy, the company aims for (1) zero new HIV infections, (2) zero employees and family members becoming sick or dying from AIDS, and (3) zero babies born HIV positive in employees' families. The program employs AIDS training staff to develop peer educators, who in turn encourage their fellow employees to expand their own knowledge of AIDS and discuss sex openly. This approach has helped alleviate the stigma associated with AIDS victims and patients. Condoms are distributed free of charge, and treatment is provided for sexually transmitted infections. The company's senior leadership has also taken a leading role in rolling out its programs, even publicly taking HIV tests.[7]

In order to achieve the three zeros, Anglo American encourages all of its employees to know their own serostatus and seeks to maintain an accurate understanding of the impact of HIV on company operations. Knowledge of serostatus among employees helps prevent further infections and enables timely treatment and care. According to Brian Brink, senior vice president of health services at Anglo American, employee HIV testing not only provides employees with valuable information, it also motivates them to modify their own behavior. In that spirit, Anglo American offers free VCT for its employees and their family members.

4. Anglo American, *Report to Society 2005* (London: Anglo American, 2006), 45.
5. Anglo American, *Report to Society 2006* (London: Anglo American, 2007), 27.
6. Anglo American, *Report to Society 2006*, 26.
7. Anglo American, "Anglo American Chiefs Leading the Way on HIV and AIDS," December 3, 2007, www.angloamerican.co.uk/aa/media/releases/2007pr/2007-12-03/.

A year after the company launched its VCT program in 2002, fewer than 10 percent of its employees in South Africa had undergone testing. By 2005, while the company's testing rates around the world had only risen to 31 percent, its best-performing mines in South Africa were seeing testing rates that exceeded 90 percent, with the Goedehoop branch achieving a testing rate of 96 percent. By 2007, more than 70 percent of employees in "risk areas" around the world had undergone testing and the company had also launched a major campaign to encourage all of its employees to be tested, including those working at its London headquarters.[8] Annual targets for VCT uptake are set and managers are also held accountable for performance, just as they would be for other work-related activities.[9] In order to improve the consultation rate, the company has put confidentiality measures in place, is providing treatment and care for employees who test positive, and is working to safeguard HIV-positive employees from discrimination.

Prevention

Training of peer educators

Internal and external trainers provide training to employees who are interested in becoming peer educators, and the latter encourage their fellow employees to expand their knowledge of AIDS and to discuss sex openly. This approach has also helped alleviate the stigma associated with HIV infection. AIDS-related information and condoms are informally distributed through these employees. Employees trained as peer educators receive proactive training in behavior modification in addition to AIDS education.

Education

HIV/AIDS prevention information and educational programs are provided to all employees and are tailored to their levels of education and literacy as well as to their culture and customs. Upon joining the company and after any extended vacations, all employees receive mandatory training that encompasses AIDS-related topics, including information on AIDS, other sexually transmitted infections, and tuberculosis; Anglo American and government policies; and facilities where employees can obtain counseling. In addition, executives receive mandatory training in the evaluation

8. Anglo American, *Report to Society 2007*, 33.
9. Business Action for Africa, *Business and HIV/AIDS: What Have we Learnt?* www.businessactionforafrica.org/documents/BAABusinessandHIVAIDS.pdf.

and management of Anglo American AIDS programs, infection status confidentiality, the legal framework for any breaches of confidentiality, and changes in health conditions resulting from treatment.

Free distribution of condoms

Anglo American distributes condoms within the company at in-house clinics, as well as at local bars, hotels, and cafes associated with commercial sex. Most condoms are provided at no charge by the government or a nongovernmental organization (NGO) and are in turn distributed free of charge by Anglo American. At certain sites, commercial sex workers trained as peer educators are responsible for promoting safe sex and distributing condoms.

ARV treatment

Mines are generally located far from urban centers, offering poor access to formal medical institutions. As a result, mining companies in South Africa have traditionally been equipped with facilities to provide health and medical services to their employees. Anglo American follows this rule, providing medical services to all employees through in-house clinics managed by Aurum Health Research. In August 2002, the company adopted company-funded ARV treatment as part of its treatment program for HIV-infected employees.

Although Anglo American was one of the first companies to introduce ARV treatment, it encountered numerous challenges before reaching the decision. It was Dr. Brink who strongly advocated the need to launch the ARV treatment program and eventually convinced his colleagues to allow a pilot project in 2001. At the time, many officers were aware of the necessity for ARV treatment, but they initially objected to its in-house provision for a variety of reasons.

First, there was the problem of costs. Annual treatment costs were about twice the annual wages for a mine worker. Because Anglo American provides medical services in-house, it had to shoulder the cost of purchasing drugs and the cost of building and maintaining a system for providing continuous treatment. The South Africa National Mining Association also expressed concerns about providing ARV at Anglo American, insisting on a commitment to long-term continuous treatment.[10]

The question of who was entitled to receive treatment was another major problem. At the time, government medical institutions did not yet provide

10. CNN.com, "AIDS: 20 Years of an Epidemic."

ARV. This meant that while employees were able to receive ARV treatment, other family members without company medical insurance were not. Since one family tended to have more than one person living with HIV/AIDS, there was concern that the system would create disparities among the employees' family members in terms of access to treatment.

Once begun, ARV treatment cannot be stopped, so there needed to be an appropriate infrastructure in place to continue treatment for employees following their retirement from active employment. Other challenges included the difficulty of taking drugs twice daily at the work site without attracting the attention of coworkers.

Despite these difficulties, Dr. Brink continued to pursue his efforts, assisted by some encouraging developments. First, the cost of ARV drugs began to decline. Under growing international criticism of the high cost of these medications, which was significantly hindering access to treatment in developing countries, the flexibility of the Trade-Related Aspects of Intellectual Property Rights (TRIPS) Agreement was codified in 2001 at the Doha Ministerial Conference in a Declaration on the TRIPS Agreement and Public Health. As awareness of the AIDS crisis mounted, major companies doing business in regions with high infection rates came under increasing pressure to take action. A 2001 survey by Anglo American showed that the absence of AIDS countermeasures, such as the provision of ARV treatment, would add €6 in costs per ounce of gold mined, with the total cost for the whole company estimated to amount to €911,000 per year. On the other hand, the cost of providing ARV to employees and their family members who needed it was estimated at €408,000 for the first year.[11] Armed with that information, Anglo American's CEO Tony Trahar announced at an executive meeting held on August 1, 2002, his decision to provide ARV treatment to all HIV-infected employees in South Africa with a simple, resolute announcement of "Let's do it!"

The cost of treatment varied from region to region within South Africa and from group company to group company. In the first year of ARV provision, treatment costs for each patient reached a monthly average of 1,234 rand (US$194). Two years later, monthly costs at some companies had dropped to 915 rand (US$144) per patient. The reasons for this drop included a decline in the cost of ARV drugs and the ability to purchase

11. Statement made by Joelle Tanguy, managing director of the Global Business Coalition on HIV/AIDS, at a Friends of the Global Fund, Japan, symposium on "The Role of Business in the Fight Against AIDS, Tuberculosis, and Malaria," June 28, 2005.

them in bulk, resulting from increased consultation rates that detected increased numbers of infected employees. Of special note is that Anglo American contracted with GlaxoSmithKline to purchase medicine at prices given to nonprofit organizations (one-tenth the normal price in industrialized countries) through Aurum Health Research. The cost of providing ARV treatment is reportedly offset by reductions in costs related to losses arising from absenteeism or medical services (particularly hospitalization), as well as the cost of training new employees.[12] According to 2007 estimates, 26 percent of the 13,886 estimated infected employees received ARV treatment, of whom 95 percent were able to continue working normally.[13]

In November 2003, the South African cabinet decided to introduce ARV treatment through the public sector, allowing people with national health insurance to receive ARV treatment for free at official medical institutions. However, various challenges—notably infrastructure problems—meant that many people were still unable to receive adequate treatment. It is for that reason that Anglo American decided to continue its program in South Africa to guarantee that its HIV-positive employees could continue receiving life-saving treatment.

Also worth noting is that, while up until 2008 treatment at Anglo American was limited to dependent family members of employees who had company health insurance, an alarming rise in new HIV/AIDS infections coupled with multidrug-resistant tuberculosis led Anglo American to announce in June of that year that it would provide its AIDS program to all of its employees and their families. Miners are at particular risk of contracting silicosis, a respiratory ailment caused by dust, and studies have shown that this disease, when combined with HIV infection, made people 12 times more likely to develop active tuberculosis in their lungs. With both diseases putting a strain on an already weak national health system, Brink in an interview with the *Times* of South Africa said the company would set up company clinics staffed with doctors and nurses that would hopefully partner with the Department of Health.[14]

Extension to communities

In order to promote AIDS programs in the workplace, one cannot overlook contacts between employees and people in the communities

12. Anglo American, *Report to Society 2005*, 46.
13. Anglo American, *Report to Society 2007*, 33.
14. "'Perfect Storm' of AIDS and TB Lashes Workers," *Times*, June 2, 2008.

where they live and work. Through its training of peer educators, Anglo American provided prevention programs and treatment for HIV/AIDS and other sexually transmitted infections—not just for employees but also for others in their communities. At the Lebowa mine in South Africa, where Anglo Platinum operates, the company also paid the cost of tuition for 12 women entering nursing school who had worked as peer educators under Anglo American's Community AIDS Program in order to help deal with the serious shortage of nurses.

Since the 1970s, as part of its social responsibility initiatives, Anglo American has supported community activities in South Africa through the creation of the Anglo American Chairman's Fund. In 2003, a total of some 73.5 million rand (approximately US$10.2 million) was granted to 450 projects. The fund emphasizes education, but it also supports AIDS-related activities including prevention education, community-based care, income-generation activities, and care for AIDS orphans.

In August 2003, the fund launched its Anglo American Community HIV and AIDS Partnership Program to support AIDS-prevention education activities within communities, with the goal of enhancing the impact of HIV/AIDS workplace programs. In the first three years, 30 million rand (US$4.7 million) was granted to Love Life, an NGO implementing AIDS-prevention education activities for youth. At the same time, the Global Fund also began providing "joint investment" financing for Love Life as a way to promote public-private partnerships. Love Life took in around 100 leaders of youth groups in the eight regions where Anglo American operates for one-year internships as "ground breakers"—individuals responsible for implementing afterschool AIDS prevention programs for youth in various communities. As a supplemental part of the program, Love Life established youth AIDS prevention social franchises (social programs that are replicated based on the franchising practice in the business sector) in 10 locations. In addition, the Youth-Friendly Clinic Initiative was created to provide services at official clinics in the communities to other residents, including youth. In concert with Love Life, Anglo American began offering not only financial support to their target communities but also specialized knowledge and expertise related to the fight against AIDS. Anglo American reportedly expects that the initiative will lead to cooperation between the medical service programs provided by Anglo American, including ARV treatment, and regional public medical services. The program has also been expanded to include Power Belt—a coalition among all of the coalmines within the Highveld region—and the Project Support Association, which focuses on Goedehoop workplace peer educators and their activities in the community.[15]

The Anglo American Community HIV and AIDS Partnership Program also receives funding from the President's Emergency Plan for AIDS Relief of the United States to support home-based care for AIDS orphans and widows through other NGOs.

In December 2007, coinciding with World AIDS Day, the Sishen mine in South Africa, which is operated by Anglo American's Kumba Iron Ore, opened the Ulysses Gogi Modise Wellness Centre, the only privately sponsored clinic in the Northern Cape Province. In addition to VCT and education, it also provides ARV treatment. This clinic represents a partnership between Kumba Iron Ore, the local municipality, and the provincial Department of Health. Kumba sponsored the costs of establishing the center and will pay all operating costs through 2010 at a cost of US$2.5 million. The goal is to then transfer ownership and management of the Wellness Centre to the Department of Health.[16]

Monitoring and evaluation

In 2003, Anglo American launched its Socio-Economic Assessment Toolbox (SEAT) as a tool to involve and engage external stakeholders, including employees' families, community organizations, other businesses, and local government agencies to "address and improve local development impacts" in the areas of its operations. Working with external actors, the toolbox helps set key performance indicators for various issues related to a specific branch of the company and creates targets for those indicators and mechanisms to regularly evaluate outcomes. In areas of high risk for HIV/AIDS, such as the Goedehoop mine in South Africa, health indicators and targets within the SEAT framework are set by the management team and other stakeholders, including community organizations and the Department of Health. New assessments are run every three years, and training sessions are held for large numbers of senior managers and NGO partners on how to use SEAT for maximum impact. According to Anglo American's website, for example, more than

15. Anglo Coal, *Goedehoop Colliery Socio-Economic Assessment Toolbox Report*, www.angloamerican.co.uk/aa/development/society/engagement/seat/acsa_seat_report_29sep05.pdf.
16. Anglo American, *Report to Society 2007*, 34.

200 people participated in SEAT workshops held in 2007 in Australia, Brazil, Peru, and South Africa.[17]

In 2007, the group went a step further. In a widely praised move, it made SEAT publicly available through its website for any company or civil society organization to use free of charge in its monitoring and evaluation processes.[18] By taking this results-oriented approach to reducing the negative impact of HIV/AIDS, Anglo American brought to the forefront the need not only to address the processes of HIV/AIDS programs but to make the regular monitoring and evaluation of outcomes a necessary part of taking action.

In developing countries with underdeveloped medical infrastructure, it is often difficult to determine whether the government or companies are responsible for protecting employee health and increasing productivity. The example of Anglo American shows that a company can eventually improve its own bottom line through a bold program for preventing HIV infection and treating HIV-positive employees and family members. It has also shown that determined corporate leadership can contribute by prompting governmental responses as well.

17. Anglo American, "Socio-Economic Assessment Toolbox," www.angloamerican.co.uk/aa/development/society/engagement/seat.

18. Keynote speech by Anglo American CEO, Cynthia Carroll, at the Business for Social Responsibility Annual Conference, October 24, 2007.

The Coca-Cola Company
Leveraging Networks to Fight AIDS

The birth of the Coca-Cola Company dates back to 1886, when an Atlanta, Georgia, pharmacist, Dr. John Styth Pemberton, concocted a mixture of sugar, water, caffeine, and extracts from coca leaves and kola nuts. In the 120 years since the creation of the Coca-Cola concentrate, the company has expanded to become the world's number one maker of soft drinks, offering nearly 2,800 beverage products in more than 200 countries worldwide. Coca-Cola became available in South Africa as early as 1929, but it was during World War II, in 1943, that the first bottling plant was opened in Algiers to help provide beverages to combat areas in Europe and lift the morale of the American troops. The presence of the company has since expanded in Africa, and today it operates throughout the continent's 56 countries and territories. Together with its bottling partners, it now employs some 55,000 staff, making it Africa's largest consumer-products employer.

According to the Joint UN Programme on HIV/AIDS, of the estimated 39 million people infected with HIV worldwide, approximately 70 percent live in Africa. HIV/AIDS is a serious threat to Africa's social and economic development and is also an urgent issue affecting all Coca-Cola operations in Africa. A healthy workforce, together with a growing economic market, is essential to the company's business. The company's HIV/AIDS program not only covers its employees but also extends prevention and treatment to all of its employees' dependents, partner companies' employees, and their dependents. It offers the largest health service program in the private sector in Africa, making the most of its huge production and distribution infrastructure.

Types of activities related to HIV/AIDS

- Workplace HIV/AIDS program promoting awareness and offering prevention education, voluntary counseling and testing (VCT), treatment, care, and support to all employees of the company and its bottling partners and their dependents

- Funding to community HIV/AIDS-related programs
- Cooperation with nongovernmental organizations (NGOs) and international organizations using its extensive distribution network and public relations infrastructure

Coca-Cola in Africa and Its HIV/AIDS Program

The impact of the HIV/AIDS pandemic on Coca-Cola's operations became increasingly visible in South Africa in the mid-1990s, as the number of employees complaining of health disorders, missing work, taking long-term sick leave, and dying because of AIDS started to increase. Others were taking time off from work to attend funerals for family members and friends. According to a calculation made by the Coca-Cola Company in South Africa, each additional case of HIV/AIDS costs eight times the annual earnings of the individual when one takes into account medical expenses, sick leave, absenteeism, and recruitment, training, and wages for a substitute worker or temporary labor. At first, no one at Coca-Cola had any idea how to handle the situation, but there was general agreement that something needed to be done—even at some cost—for the long-term benefit of the business.

In November 2000, the company developed the Coca-Cola Africa Group HIV/AIDS Charter and launched an HIV/AIDS program for its approximately 8,000 employees and their dependents in South Africa. To ensure accurate knowledge of HIV/AIDS, the company organizes regular meetings and recreational activities to educate and inform employees about HIV/AIDS. Peer educators chosen from among the employees are trained to provide their colleagues with counseling and support. Free condoms are also distributed at the events.

The company promotes community involvement in part through its "Big Match," an internal employee program that matches funds donated or raised by employees for HIV/AIDS community initiatives of their choice. Employees may also take time off to volunteer in HIV/AIDS and other charitable community outreach activities with company sponsorship and support.

Employees and their family members are encouraged to undergo confidential VCT for HIV/AIDS, which is conducted through a partnership with onsite occupational health clinics, external third party service providers, government institutions, and NGOs. Full antiretroviral (ARV) treatment, care, and support are provided when deemed necessary through a comprehensive company medical aid program to HIV-infected employees and family members who have been tested and are willing to participate in the program.

In order to monitor and evaluate the success of the workplace program, both quantitative and qualitative data from all key locations are gathered on a quarterly basis through a formal evaluation and data collection process. Program information is gathered by regular internal reports, which include information on minimum standards of sustenance, ARV uptake, number of VCT coupons redeemed, number of education and awareness sessions conducted, employee participation levels, healthcare costs, feedback on community outreach activities, mortality statistics, absenteeism, and number of condoms distributed. Behavioral information is also gathered through occasional surveys of knowledge, attitudes, and practices. All the information is used to generate reports and statistical analyses that are shared with the leadership teams and used to improve the program itself.

The cost of carrying out the above program activities is covered through the employee benefits program. To further increase program utilization, the Coca-Cola Africa Foundation was established in 2001 and headquartered in Swaziland, with a commitment to supporting the local bottling partners by cofunding the start-up costs of the HIV/AIDS workplace program. As explained below, the company extends financial assistance to all its bottling partners to help them set up a similar program in their workplace.

Expanding the Program throughout the Entire Coca-Cola System in Africa

Coca-Cola operates on a unique production and distribution system comprised of the company and its network of bottlers, referred to as the "Coca-Cola system." The company manufactures concentrate, beverage bases, and syrups that are sold to its licensed and franchised bottling partners around the world. The bottling partners then combine the concentrate with carbonated water, sweetener, or both; produce and package the finished beverages in authorized containers; sell them to customers; and take care of recycling the containers. Aside from manufacturing the concentrates, a significant portion of the company's work focuses on creating and marketing its brands. The Coca-Cola system has more than 300 bottling partners and 800 bottling plants worldwide. Most of these are not owned or managed by the company but rather are independent companies operating locally.

In November 2002, two years after the rollout of Coca-Cola's HIV/AIDS workplace program for its employees and their families in Africa, the target of the program was expanded to include all 40 of the bottling partners throughout the continent. The expansion ensured that all the employees and their spouses and children in the Coca-Cola system in Africa would have access to HIV prevention education and to ARV treatment and care as required. The move originated in the conviction that equal access to the same level of care, as set forth in the company's HIV/AIDS Charter created in 2000, was necessary in order to minimize the impact of HIV/AIDS on its business. The problem was how to finance the expanded coverage. Since the company cannot offer healthcare coverage to its bottling partners, who are managed independently, the Coca-Cola Africa Foundation stepped in to reimburse up to 50 percent of the costs of the bottling partners' HIV/AIDS programs.

Most of the implementation of the workplace program for the bottling partners is conducted in conjunction with regional branches of international NGOs or local volunteer groups. More recently, alliance with the Network of African People Living with HIV/AIDS has brought the perspective of HIV-positive individuals into the program. By having people living with HIV/AIDS cooperate as technical advisors, participants in the educational programs have been able to learn from their experiences and more fully understand the gravity of the issue.

Before the company decided to expand the program to all of its bottling partners, only two of the partners had any programs of their own. Now, with all of the bottling partners involved, beneficiaries of the program have expanded to include approximately 360,000 employees and dependents. The foundation has also been organizing forums that gather the various bottling partners in order for them to exchange information and share their experiences.

Distribution Network as Core Competency

An important core competency of the Coca-Cola Company is its marketing expertise and expansive distribution network. On a continent where the transportation system is not well developed, the delivery trucks and storage facilities belonging to members of the Coca-Cola system permit community access to condoms and other prevention and awareness materials. For example, one of the bottling partners in Zambia offered support to the Society for Family Health (SFH), a subsidiary of Population Services International, by using its infrastructure to store and deliver medication, equipment, supplies, and educational materials. The local Zambian bottler utilized its extensive distribution network, as well as its fleet of delivery and sales trucks, to distribute condoms and disseminate educational pamphlets throughout the country. The services offered by the Zambian bottler are conducted as part of the overall HIV/AIDS program in the workplace, which also includes maintenance of testing and counseling centers in the manufacturing factories, awareness programs for management and regular employees, and community outreach activities. The cooperation has permitted SFH to reach 70 percent of the entire country.

Another core competency of a worldwide corporation like Coca-Cola is the great impact it can have through advertising. The company has cooperated with the United Nations Children's Fund to promote an HIV/AIDS awareness-raising program for youth in Nigeria by providing free airing of President Obasanjo's message on the radio and free advertising space on outdoor billboards. Such advertisements can easily reach young people, who are the target of the messages, because of the strong support the company enjoys among the youth.

From "African Initiative" to a Global Corporate Commitment

Coca-Cola has made clear commitments to corporate responsibility, focusing its work in four areas: marketplace, workplace, community, and environment. The company describes its mandate as a global corporate citizen as being to market its products responsibly, treat its employees fairly, make a difference in the communities where it does business, and protect the environment in which everyone lives and works. The issue of

HIV/AIDS falls under the workplace pillar, along with workplace rights, human rights, employee relations, safety, and diversity.

In 2005, Coca-Cola began to expand its HIV/AIDS activities to other regions. The senior vice president responsible for human resources assigned a human resources executive to develop a global toolkit that would assist in the transfer of the lessons learned in Africa to other regions at risk from the disease. Pilot efforts have been launched in three countries: China, India, and Russia. Coca-Cola China even sent a delegation of staff and local foundation representatives to visit its South African counterpart to learn more about its workplace HIV/AIDS programs and community activities. The company has since strengthened its local nondiscrimination policy in the workplace in China. In addition, the company has embarked on a campaign of cooperation with the Chinese Foundation for the Prevention of STDs and AIDS to raise awareness and promote prevention. The campaign aims to distribute educational materials to 50 million people across more than 100 cities in China. This prevention initiative, together with other contributions made as a part of Coca-Cola's commitment to corporate responsibility, has won Coca-Cola China numerous awards. In Russia, partnerships with local NGOs are rolling out HIV/AIDS programs similar to those offered in Africa. In India, human resources professionals underwent training as HIV/AIDS counselors in order to begin implementing a workplace awareness program in 2007.

Coca-Cola's experience illustrates how a company's various core competencies and wide-reaching networks can be leveraged creatively in the fight against HIV/AIDS.

Interviews

David Brown, Director, Global Employee Relations Strategy, Coca-Cola Company (headquarters)
Angela Ho, Manager, Community Affairs, Coca-Cola South Africa
Audri Riffel, Manager, Human Resources, Coca-Cola South Africa

DaimlerChrysler South Africa
A Model for Public-Private Partnership

As one of the largest automotive companies in the world, DaimlerChrysler operates plants in 37 countries and sells cars in more than 200 countries around the world.[1] Headquartered in Germany, it employs more than 360,000 people globally. The company's AIDS measures were initiated by DaimlerChrysler South Africa (DCSA), a production base for Mercedes-Benz automobiles that has three branches: Pinetown in Kwazulu-Natal (parts); Pretoria in Gauteng (management and sales); and East London in Eastern Cape (production). As of 2007, DCSA had approximately 3,200 employees and roughly 3,000 suppliers.

DCSA established its first HIV/AIDS guidelines for its workplaces in 1996. Since 2000, more comprehensive AIDS programs have been implemented in partnership with GTZ (Deutsche Gesellschaft für Technische Zusammenarbeit), Germany's official aid organization, and these programs have become models for public-private partnership in the HIV/AIDS field. In 2004, DaimlerChrysler decided to extend its South African model to its worldwide production bases.

Types of activities related to HIV/AIDS

- Workplace policy to eliminate discrimination against HIV-positive employees and ensure confidentiality of serostatus
- Peer educator approach to implementing awareness-raising activities aimed at behavior change for all employees
- Awareness raising through web-based information and events
- Voluntary counseling and testing (VCT) services with incentives

1. Daimler-Benz and the Chrysler Corporation merged in 1998, forming DaimlerChrysler AG. The group later sold Chrysler in May 2007. Most of the research for this chapter was undertaken before the sale of Chrysler, so the information pertains to the larger group of companies—DaimlerChrysler AG—prior to the sale.

for employees to participate in VCT and for healthcare workers to provide VCT services
- Condom promotion and distribution
- Treatment for HIV-positive employees and family members, including antiretroviral (ARV) treatment and prevention of mother-to-child transmission
- Work reassignment for employees who are no longer able to perform current work duties due to AIDS-related illness and compensation for those who are not able to continue working
- Partnership with GTZ and the National Union of Metalworkers of South Africa (NUMSA)
- International advocacy on HIV/AIDS
- Detailed monitoring and evaluation of HIV/AIDS-related activities

Background and Evolution

DCSA began to feel the impact of HIV/AIDS in the early 1990s, when it began to lose skilled labor due to infected employees' absences. The first confirmed death of a DCSA employee from AIDS occurred in 1992. This prompted a discussion among health service representatives, executives, and NUMSA officials about how the company should deal with this disease, leading it to establish its first workplace policy on HIV/AIDS in 1996. The policy called for the elimination of discrimination against infected employees and highlighted the importance of awareness and education in the workplace. It also covered healthcare services at the workplace, provision of AIDS-related information and education opportunities, distribution of condoms, provision of treatment for sexually transmitted infections and tuberculosis, AIDS-related consultation and support, and efforts to promote employee health. Nevertheless, according to Dr. Clifford Panter, DCSA's AIDS program coordinator, until around 1999 these specific AIDS-related activities were mere stopgap measures.

As HIV infection spread rapidly throughout South Africa, AIDS became the leading cause of death among DCSA employees in 1998. At that time, the company recognized that if it was going to maintain a stable investment and manufacturing environment in South Africa, it would have to make an institutional commitment to fighting AIDS. In 1999, DCSA's healthcare plan, DCMed, contracted with Medscheme, a major manager of health schemes in South Africa, to use the services of a Medscheme subsidiary, the Aid for AIDS (AFA) program, in exchange for a corporate membership fee. DCSA employees can decide whether or not to enroll in the AFA program without having to notify DCSA or DCMed directly, and the bill that DCMed receives from the AFA program does not include names of recipients, which protects their rights to confidentiality regarding their serostatus. Employees who enroll in the program can choose from among a selection of medical facilities recommended by the AFA program, including the in-company clinic.

One would think that the grave picture painted of the potential impact of HIV/AIDS on a manufacturing company like DCSA would have simply driven such a company out of South Africa. Instead, the company decided in 2000 to strengthen and consolidate its workplace program on HIV/AIDS to be more strategically managed, monitored, and evaluated, which has helped the program to successfully mitigate the impact of HIV/AIDS on DCSA operations. Although the company estimated in 2002 that HIV/AIDS-related expenditures would peak at 4 percent of total salary expenses,[2] the disease has had no noticeable impact on company profits. In fact, the success of its HIV/AIDS program was one of several factors that the board of DaimlerChrysler Management considered in deciding to substantially reinvest in manufacturing and in wholesale and retail sales in South Africa.

Activities

The following section covers DCSA's HIV/AIDS programs between 2000 and 2007.

Partnership with GTZ

Around the year 2000, companies in South Africa began to express alarm over the rising costs associated with AIDS, as direct costs attributable to AIDS were projected to double over the coming 5 to 10 years. When the indirect costs associated with absenteeism, the loss of skilled labor, and the cost of training and recruiting new employees were added, the projected costs became even more formidable. The burden of medical costs and loss of labor due to AIDS weighed heavily on DCSA, which recognized that it would eventually need to form partnerships with third

2. World Economic Forum, "Global Health Initiative: Private Sector Intervention Case Example, DaimlerChrysler, 2002," www.weforum.org/pdf/Initiatives/GHI_HIV_CaseStudy_DCSA.pdf.

parties in order to effectively manage labor and productivity through more systematic AIDS measures.

Around the end of the 1990s, Germany's Federal Ministry for Economic Cooperation and Development (BMZ) began seeking out partnerships with the corporate sector in developing countries as a result of modest increases in its aid budget. Around the same time, German companies were rapidly increasing their investment in developing countries, and the aid agency personnel had high expectations that such investment would result in job creation in and technology transfers to developing countries. In 1999, BMZ tentatively established a fund for promoting public-private partnerships over a period of three years and commissioned GTZ and KfW Bankengruppe (Germany's development bank) to implement the project. As a part of that project, GTZ approached DCSA about the possibility of forming a public-private partnership, and in July 2000, with the consent of the labor union, GTZ and DCSA decided to implement the company's first AIDS program through that partnership.

Project details

The nature of the project was determined through consultations with various concerned parties: DCSA's management and employees, GTZ, NUMSA, and medical personnel. The HIV/AIDS policy was revised and specified the following: (1) elimination of discrimination against HIV-positive people in recruitment and layoffs; (2) confidentiality of serostatus; (3) compensation depending on serostatus; (4) compensation for those forced to leave employment due to medical problems caused by the onset of AIDS; and (5) assured access to DCSA's HIV/AIDS programs for contractors and suppliers. In addition to the policy, three new programs were instituted: (1) reconstitution of the current medical services into a more comprehensive system that also covers sexually transmitted infections and tuberculosis; (2) revision of the healthcare benefit system for ARV treatment provision and revision of the personnel system to minimize the impact of absenteeism, loss of employment, and productivity slowdowns; and (3) promotion of AIDS awareness and education. The primary goal of the project was to reduce the burden on the medical service and personnel departments, which found their workloads increasing as the rates of people infected with HIV were growing annually.

In order to improve the program's implementation and monitoring, an HIV/AIDS Task Force composed of about 20 members was created in

July 2001 with representatives from management, the labor union, and the medical staff of DCSA, as well as from GTZ. Dr. Clifford Panter, an occupational health consultant for the East London branch, was appointed HIV/AIDS program coordinator for the entire program. The total budget for the project's four-year period was estimated at US$600,000, of which DCSA bore 80 percent and GTZ 20 percent. The project was primarily led by DCSA, with GTZ providing support for surveys and analyses. GTZ also brought nongovernmental organizations (NGOs), research institutes, and international organizations from its network into the partnership and promoted program management skills. Project implementation required cooperation among central and state governments, national economic organizations (such as the South Africa Chamber of Commerce and Industry and the South African Business Coalition on HIV and AIDS), NUMSA, the Congress of South African Trade Unions, and the Joint United Nations Programme on HIV/AIDS.

In the first stage, the project's principal targets were male employees ranging in age from 20 to 49. In the second stage, it was expanded to include other employees, family members, residents in the project area, suppliers, contractors, and retailers.

Needs assessment and monitoring

With technical support provided by GTZ, knowledge, attitude, perceptions, and behavior (KAP/B) surveys of employees were undertaken to determine DCSA employees' AIDS-related risks. The results of the survey indicated that many employees lacked accurate knowledge of AIDS. In particular, information concerning the treatment scheme provided by DCSA was not widely known, and there was a strong fear of AIDS-related stigma and discrimination, along with a low level of awareness of sexually transmitted infections. In October 2001, using methodology developed by the Centers for Disease Control and Prevention in the United States and the World Health Organization (WHO), researchers at the Durban Medical Research Council and the WHO surveyed HIV prevalence in DCSA branches in Pinetown, Pretoria, and East London. With roughly 80 percent of the employees in the three branches participating, the survey indicated an average infection rate of 9 percent, which was somewhat lower than in surrounding areas.

KAP/B studies and infection rate surveys are conducted at regular intervals so that the AIDS program can be adjusted as needed. This system of monitoring was intended to place the AIDS program at the core of DCSA activities.

Provision of comprehensive medical services

Treatment of tuberculosis and sexually transmitted infections was explicitly incorporated into AIDS treatment programs, because numerous AIDS patients died of tuberculosis and because individuals with sexually transmitted infections are more susceptible to HIV infection. As noted above, ARV treatment has been provided through Medscheme's AFA program since 1999. The AFA program provides treatment to those subscribing employees and their family members whose CD4 levels have declined enough to make them eligible for treatment. DCSA purchases the ARV treatment that is provided through the AFA program at a reduced price through GTZ.

South Africans who test positive for HIV infection have been eligible for treatment under the national healthcare scheme since 2004, but the AFA program offers several advantages over the national scheme. The AFA program allows for earlier access to treatment and offers greater support to prevent mother-to-child transmission. It also offers more options in terms of viral load monitoring, resistance testing, and drug choices.[3]

DCSA undertakes various health promotion campaigns, including the distribution of condoms and a VCT campaign. The number of condoms distributed in the East London branch doubled from November 2000 to December 2001, and 1,750 employees were tested from 2001 through October 2002. During the VCT campaign period, launched in May 2002 and again in 2005/2006, everyone who participated received a letter from the chairman and a small gift, and their names were entered into a lottery for cash prizes to increase participation rates. Since 2006, the company has shifted its policy to encourage employees' and their families' primary care physicians to conduct HIV testing and other preventive healthcare testing by offering bonuses for such services. Staff in the company clinics are also offered incentives to encourage routine HIV testing while still respecting the employee's right to opt out.

Revision of the personnel management and benefits system

In 2001, risk assessments were undertaken in order to minimize the effects of AIDS on company operations, and schemes such as death

3. Under the national scheme, those who test positive receive ARV treatment when their CD4 level goes down to 250, but the AFA program allows them to begin accessing treatment earlier, at a CD4 level of 350. HIV-positive mothers and their newborns are only given single doses of Nevirapine under the national scheme, but the AFA program offers the mothers full ARV treatment, delivers the children through caesarian section to reduce the risk of passing on infection, and provides the newborn with azidothymidine.

benefits, funeral benefits, and medical insurance were reviewed based on the results.

Subscribers to the AFA program can receive compensation of up to US$2,500 per year from the DCSA medical fund. In 2001, medical compensation received directly by AFA program subscribers (including treatment and other costs) averaged US$124 per month. However, anticipating that there would be cases that would exceed the maximum benefit, DCSA made an additional contribution of US$700,000 into the fund in 2001. Before the creation of South Africa's national HIV/AIDS treatment program, DCSA provided compensation for medical expenses to former employees who were infected while they were employed at the company so that they could continue their treatment, but few took advantage of this benefit.

HIV/AIDS prevention education and other educational activities

DCSA estimates that the prevention of HIV infection in one employee will save costs equal to three to four times the annual salary of that employee, making prevention an important priority. DCSA has a two-pronged prevention program, which includes peer educator training and information provision.

DCSA seeks to train one peer educator for every 30 employees. Peer educators are volunteers selected from among the general workforce and supplier sales personnel charged with holding monthly sessions for their coworkers at their workplace, where they provide AIDS-related information and consultations. AIDS prevention education through peer educators has been incorporated into existing workplace communication activities and training systems. Because peer educators are not compensated for the time they spend educating their fellow employees, the management tries to provide support to make their jobs easier and gets reports on their activities. Strong management support is necessary to allow employees to promote AIDS awareness at their workplaces while balancing work activities and other responsibilities. As of October 2002, 180 peer educators had been trained from among 4,453 employees, of whom 55 percent were still engaged in their activities as of 2007.

"Info-Island" computer touch screen kiosks have been installed at each branch to provide AIDS-related information in an entertaining format in the languages of the major ethnic groups. In addition, a helpline has been instituted to provide consultations on HIV/AIDS. AIDS prevention education is also provided through workplace communication activities, training systems, and health promotion campaigns. During the VCT campaign, special emphasis was placed on compensation and services available for those testing positive for HIV. For blue-collar workers, awareness-raising activities associated with campaigns or events have proven particularly effective. In addition, eight nurses trained in AIDS counseling by the Health Department offer personal counseling on HIV risk and testing.

However, despite such AIDS education efforts, no HIV-positive employees have disclosed their serostatus to their peers, despite estimates that some 400 employees were infected as of October 2002. This reflects the fact that discussion of sexuality remains a deeply ingrained taboo in South African society and is also a sign of the strong stigma still attached to AIDS in this region of the world.

Extension to communities

Since 2006, DCSA employees have started asking their doctors in the local clinics to conduct HIV testing, leading DCSA to develop a policy to provide financial incentives for the doctors who provide testing. In addition, DCSA supports other community-based AIDS-related activities in order to extend the HIV/AIDS programs that it already offers to its employees and their family members to the communities where it operates as well. Since 2004, DCSA has actively supported neighboring communities in cooperation with public hospitals and schools. Grants made in 2006 included the Siyakhana project of the Border-Kei Chamber of Business in East London, a public-private partnership with Deutsche Investitions und Entwicklungsgesellschaft (a member of the KfW Bankengruppe) designed to strengthen HIV/AIDS-related activities in small- and medium-sized enterprises and to support hospices and home care in Pretoria.

Impact

The HIV/AIDS program implemented in partnership with GTZ was generally effective in terms of prevention and treatment and raising VCT rates. In addition, through GTZ, DCSA learned new project management skills; gained experience with epidemiological analysis, medical methodology, and reporting methods; gained access to networks with internal and international institutes; and learned about future issues and information on funding sources. More concretely, as noted above, the number of condoms distributed in the East London branch doubled from November 2000 to December 2001, and 1,750 employees were tested from 2001 through October 2002.

When the scheme was initiated in 1999, there were no AFA subscribers in DCSA, but by April 2007, an estimated 256 employees were HIV positive, 201 of whom were enrolled in the disease management program, with an additional 123 family members in the program as well. Of these, 114 employees and 37 family members were receiving ARV treatment. Since 1999, a total of 85 women employees and 135 women family members have taken advantage of services to prevent mother-to-child transmission. As of 2007, none of the subscribers had died; only 12 faced medical problems that made it difficult for them to continue working, and the majority of them were expected to return to work. An additional 5 employees' health conditions required them to be shifted to alternative work placements. Also, there had been no mother-to-child infections among subscribers. In addition to the AFA program, employees are covered by the in-house comprehensive health project and medical insurance.

A survey of the project's economic impact carried out at DCSA in 2002 reported cost reductions of 10 percent compared with cases involving no treatment. However, Dr. Panter argues that the purpose of AIDS programs is to minimize the negative impact of a lack of treatment, not to improve DCSA's bottom line. In any event, DCSA did enjoy growing recognition due to its partnership with GTZ, a model of public-private partnership, and this has undoubtedly resulted in positive publicity for the company. Jurgen Schrempp, DaimlerChrysler's CEO, is a firm believer in the importance of HIV/AIDS programs, and he and Christoph Koepke, DCSA's CEO, have spoken publicly about the challenges posed by HIV/AIDS as seen from the top, which has resulted in a high degree of international visibility.

The comprehensive HIV/AIDS programs implemented in partnership with GTZ were introduced to all branches of DaimlerChrysler in 2004. Global HIV/AIDS Guidelines were established in 2005, and they are particularly strong in China, India, Russia, and Southeast Asia, where HIV infection is spreading rapidly. Lessons from DCSA serve as an example for companies in South Africa and beyond. The significance of the partnership with GTZ lies not in its sharing of DCSA's costs, but in the provision of GTZ's program management skills and links to governments, international institutions, and NGOs. These connections allow DCSA to sustain a comprehensive HIV/AIDS program with the backing of external experts. Companies considering providing AIDS treatment to their employees can learn valuable lessons from DCSA activities, including how to plan for the outsourcing of counseling and treatment programs for infected employees; how to obtain permission for access to company treatment programs for family members of employees, suppliers, and contractors; and how to adopt policies for providing continuing compensation for employees, even after they leave their jobs, all by utilizing the private-sector AFA medical program.

Sumitomo Chemical
Saving Lives with Better Nets

Malaria claims more than a million human lives every year. More than 90 percent of the deaths are among children aged five or under, and fatalities are concentrated in sub-Saharan Africa. Despite the development of proven methods of prevention and treatment and the increase in public awareness of the risks of malaria—which has been cited alongside HIV/AIDS as a target of the Millennium Development Goals (MDGs)—the disease continues to spread. Ultimately, the most effective means of controlling malaria is to control the mosquitoes that spread the disease. With this in mind, Sumitomo Chemical, a leading Japanese chemical manufacturer, has developed a mosquito net that employs new technology to make the net last longer and provide more comfort, making it more likely that families in hot climates will use the nets effectively. Sumitomo Chemical's Olyset net has gained global recognition as a highly effective tool in fighting malaria transmission and has become widely used in developing countries in recent years. Through its business ties, Sumitomo Chemical has also developed partnerships with other actors involved in the fight against malaria, notably international organizations, and it has come up with a range of malaria-related programs through which it can apply its diverse resources to this important fight.

Types of activities related to malaria

- Development and manufacture of long-lasting mosquito nets
- Transfer of mosquito net production technology to Africa free of charge
- Advocacy, awareness raising, and financial contributions to the international campaign against malaria

Evolution of Anti-malarial Mosquito Nets

Initial stages

Sumitomo Chemical is a general chemical manufacturer whose main fields include petrochemicals and basic chemicals. With its agricultural chemical operations and its leading share of the global market for the active ingredients of household insecticides, the company has long been indirectly involved in the fight against malaria. Though malaria is not endemic to Japan, the Japanese company's insecticides have been used since the 1960s to fight malaria in developing countries. In the early days of the campaign against malaria, the World Health Organization (WHO) advocated eradication through residual spraying of insecticide on interior walls and ceilings, and Japanese official development assistance (ODA) was used to spray insecticides, including chemicals developed by Sumitomo Chemicals, throughout the developing world. However, while Japan and other donor countries made important ODA commitments to provide the insecticides, they failed to provide funds to pay people to apply the sprays.[1] For this reason, the insecticides were not necessarily applied systematically, and the malaria eradication program gradually lost steam. Sumitomo Chemical's next involvement with malaria would not come about until the 1980s.

In the mid-1980s, several academic groups published a study arguing that insecticide-treated nets (ITNs)—specifically, nets treated with pyrethroids—were effective tools for preventing malaria, and the WHO and other organizations began to focus on mosquito nets as a key means of fighting this disease. The malaria-carrying Anopheles mosquito generally bites at night, so sleeping inside a mosquito net is an effective way to avoid getting bitten, thereby avoiding infection. Even nets that have not been treated with insecticide have a certain degree of effectiveness, but if the net fails to completely enclose the sleeping area, or if it has developed tears as the result of long use, mosquitoes can enter through the openings. But, if the net is treated with insecticide (soaked so that the insecticide impregnates the net), mosquitoes alighting on it even briefly as they seek to enter through the openings will be knocked down or killed. On top of that, if such nets are used in all houses in a particular area, the mosquito population

1. Interview with Dr. Takaaki Itoh, Sumitomo Chemical.

in that area can be significantly reduced. Data show that the rate of malaria infection among those using ITNs is half that of those using untreated nets.[2]

Following the publication of this significant finding, researchers at Sumitomo Chemical's Agricultural Chemicals Research Laboratory started considering what sorts of insecticides would be suitable for soaking into the nets. As they did so, however, they ran into a number of challenges. For one thing, the insecticide would be removed when the nets were washed, meaning that they would have to be re-treated. For people in malaria-affected areas who were not accustomed to using mosquito nets, even just setting up the nets properly every day would be a major undertaking, so the researchers feared that it would be impossible to get them to regularly carry out the very troublesome task of re-treating the nets. Another challenge was that the mosquito nets that had been put on the market at that time had very fine mesh that blocked ventilation, meaning that people in hot African climates might find them uncomfortable for sleeping. So, the researchers focused on developing a net that would meet three conditions: (1) it must allow good ventilation; (2) it must maintain its insecticidal property even after washing, so as not to require re-treatment; and (3) it must retain its ability to kill insects for a long time.

During the 1980s, the laboratory developed technology for embedding chemical agents in resins, such as plastics. This was the same technology that was used to control blood-sucking flies by implanting insecticide in the ear tags used to identify cattle. During the boom years of economic growth in the latter half of this decade, many Japanese companies moved their plants to suburban locations and operated them during the night as well, leading to increased demand for materials that would keep insects from getting into manufactured products; insecticidal screens were developed in response. As part of this process, the laboratory accumulated basic data concerning such matters as the types of resins and chemical agents suited for processing into nets, the relationship between the ingredients and processing of the resins and their insecticidal effectiveness, and the speed of diffusion of insecticidal agents within resins. The development team became confident that if they applied this sort of technology to mosquito nets they would be able to produce a more effective and easy-to-use product. Dr. Takaaki Itoh, who was involved in the development project, recalls, "We succeeded by fusing the technologies

2. World Health Organization, *Malaria Vector Control and Personal Protection: Report of a WHO Study Group*, (Geneva: WHO, 2006), 7.

from two fields—resins and insecticides—that we had developed as a general chemical manufacturer."

As the result of this progress, the original Olyset net was born in 1992. The insecticide permethrin was implanted in resin, which was made into yarn and then knitted to make mosquito nets. Unlike the usual polyester netting, this new kind of net used thick polyethylene fiber, which made it very robust. By taking advantage of technology to have the chemical agent gradually seep out to replace that lost from the surface due to washing, the development team created a marketable product that would retain its insecticidal effect for at least five years. At this point, the new nets went into test use in malaria-affected regions of Asia and Africa. But they did not immediately win wide acceptance.

Recognition by the WHO and widespread use

The WHO began to promote the use of ITNs in the mid-1980s, but the Olyset net failed to draw the WHO's attention when it was first launched in 1992. The net was not well known around the world, and its price at the time seemed too high both to international institutions and to governments in the developing world.[3] Also, many within the WHO tended to steer away from products like the Olyset net that did not need to be re-treated.[4] Ordinary ITNs lose their insecticide after three to five washings, at which point they must be redipped. The WHO viewed public gatherings to regularly re-treat ITNs as an ideal opportunity for health education. With the passage of time, however, it became clear that the need to re-treat ordinary nets was interfering with the spread of their use. Collective re-treatment events were found to be a burden on residents who had to travel long distances to the re-treatment sites. Except in some small or socialist countries, where governments have carried out large-scale re-treatment programs free of charge, the re-treatment rate was never higher than 20 percent, and the average rate in Africa was particularly low, at 5 percent or less.[5]

In order to overcome this challenge, the WHO eventually began to focus on the Olyset net for its long-lasting insecticidal effect, dubbing them long-lasting insecticidal nets (LLINs). The WHO hoped that the elimination of the need for re-treatment would lead to wider use of

3. Interview with Dr. Pierre Guillet, WHO.
4. Interview with Dr. Itoh.
5. Pierre Guillet, et al., "Long-Lasting Treated Mosquito Nets: A Breakthrough in Malaria Prevention," *Bulletin of the World Health Organization*, no. 79 (2001): 998.

effective mosquito nets, and it also recognized that LLINs used less insecticide than ordinary ITNs and lessened the environmental burden by not allowing insecticides to dissolve in wash water. Even so, governments in developing countries that had become accustomed to ordinary ITNs were not quick to switch to the new type of netting. Dr. Pierre Guillet, a vector control specialist at the WHO, recalls that it took several years for the WHO, the United Nations Children's Fund (UNICEF), and national governments to become convinced that LLINs were superior to conventional ITNs.

In due course, LLIN use did indeed grow dramatically. This was due in part to patient persuasion by Dr. Guillet, but there were also a number of landmark events that helped promote the cause. First was the WHO's recommendation of the Olyset net as the first LLIN to qualify under its official Pesticides Evaluation Scheme in 2000. The second came in 2002, with the establishment of the Global Fund to Fight AIDS, Tuberculosis and Malaria (the Global Fund). As of 2010, the Global Fund had committed US$19.3 billion for approved measures in developing countries to combat major communicable diseases, of which one quarter is allocated for measures to treat and prevent malaria. In 2003, 80 percent of the ITNs ordered by governments in developing countries were of the type requiring re-treatment, and only 20 percent were LLINs. But, in 2004 these shares were reversed. Dr. Guillet sees this dramatic shift as being partially attributed to the funding provided by the Global Fund.[6] The supply of LLINs was insufficient to keep up with the resulting worldwide surge in demand and actual use of bednets so that manufacturers found that they had to greatly increase production.

Technology Transfer to Africa

Increasing production capacity

At Sumitomo Chemical, as soon as the Olyset net was developed, the company recognized that the price of the net would need to be low enough for developing countries to be able to use them widely, so it was determined that the labor-intensive nets would need to be produced somewhere with low labor costs. At first the nets were produced in small numbers within Japan, but then production in China began, and thanks to

6. Interview with Dr. Guillet.

patient technical training, 20,000 nets were produced in 1999. Following the WHO recommendation noted above, demand for Olyset nets surged, and the WHO, UNICEF, and others requested a large-scale increase in production. In response to these requests, Sumitomo Chemical increased its production capacity in Changzhou, China, undertaking full-scale production of the nets in 2002.

Production in Tanzania and the Olyset Consortium

The WHO, meanwhile, had a clear vision of its own: in order to fight malaria in Africa, where the disease takes its biggest toll, it would need a large supply of LLINs like the Olyset net, and for this purpose it wanted to have the production technology transferred to local enterprises in Africa. By having Africans engage in the manufacturing of these nets, it would also contribute to Africa's economic development.[7] The WHO's Dr. Guillet thus proposed to Sumitomo Chemical that it transfer the Olyset manufacturing technology free of charge to mosquito net makers in Africa, to which the company readily agreed. Because the market for the Olyset net was small in the context of Sumitomo Chemical's total business volume, there was no major argument over the idea of a gratis technology transfer.

The problem for Sumitomo Chemical was that it had no local production experience in Africa and no idea of how to go about finding enterprises to serve as its partners. In response to this hurdle, Dr. Guillet and others arranged for the establishment of the Olyset Consortium as a public-private partnership with seven members to support the technology transfer process. The Acumen Fund, one of the partners in the consortium, identified A to Z Textile Mills, a leading mosquito net maker in Tanzania, as a candidate manufacturer since it was the only manufacturer possessing the technology and experience in both plastic extruding and fiber spinning. The consortium deployed the strengths of its members to build a partnership with A to Z aimed at large-scale manufacturing of the Olyset net in Tanzania. Local production started in September 2003 in Arusha, Tanzania, and in 2004 production capacity

---

7. Guillet et al., "Long-Lasting Treated Mosquito Nets"; Global Health Initiative, "Public-Private Partnership Case Example: Building a Public-Private Partnership to Transfer the Technology of a Life-Saving Malaria Prevention Tool in Africa," World Economic Forum, 2006, www.acumenfund.org/uploads/assets/documents/A%20to%20Z%20Private-Public%20Partnership%20Study%20-%20Global%20Health%20Initiative_R1udShKh.pdf.

was already up to 300,000 a year. In Dr. Guillet's opinion, the key factor underlying the effort's success has been the individuals involved. He notes that, while the support of the various participating organizations was of course important, what ultimately moved the technology transfer process and led to a successful outcome was the fact that the individuals working in the partnership understood and respected each other and worked together with a strong team spirit and confidence. The roles played by the participants in this partnership are described below:

A to Z Textile Mills, located in Tanzania, is Africa's largest manufacturer of mosquito nets. It also mass-produces polyethylene products and other goods. It is responsible for the local manufacturing of Olyset nets.

Sumitomo Chemical, as the developer of the Olyset net, supplies the manufacturing technology free of charge and recommends the most appropriate extrusion and knitting machinery for use in manufacturing. It also supplies resins containing insecticide and conducts overall quality control of local manufacturing.

The **Acumen Fund** is a public-interest venture fund established with capital from the Rockefeller Foundation and other sources. It selected A to Z as the investment target in Africa and lent US$325,000 for investment in equipment in the first year of production. In 2005, it provided a second funding package of US$675,000 (a loan of US$400,000 and a grant of US$275,000) for expansion of production facilities and development of the distribution network.

ExxonMobil, a major US-based oil company, was originally going to provide virgin resin from a plant in Saudi Arabia to A to Z, which would in turn blend it with resin with a high level of insecticide content, which was to be supplied to it by Sumitomo Chemical. This original framework was not implemented, however, because it was found that the virgin resin was not suited to the manufacturing of Olyset nets. Nonetheless, ExxonMobil has donated US$250,000 to UNICEF to procure and distribute mosquito nets and has also supported a program for the nationwide distribution of mosquito nets in Cameroon.

UNICEF is principally responsible for buying the nets produced through the partnership and distributing them directly to low-income families. UNICEF has been promoting the use of LLINs, and it distributes Olyset nets directly to groups at high risk of contracting malaria through hospitals and maternity clinics. It has also worked with the malaria program implemented by the government of Tanzania—with financial support from the Global Fund—to promote the establishment of a voucher system for mosquito nets in that country. UNICEF is also supporting increased global production of LLINs by providing a steady flow of procurement orders.

Population Services International (PSI) is an international NGO specializing in issues related to population and public health. It has worked to promote the Olyset net as a commercially viable product through such activities as market research of African consumers; research on sales channels, including retail outlets; and advertising of the Olyset net on radio programs.

The **WHO** acts as the overall coordinator of the partnership and offers technical advice on such matters as the insecticidal effect and safety of the mosquito nets.

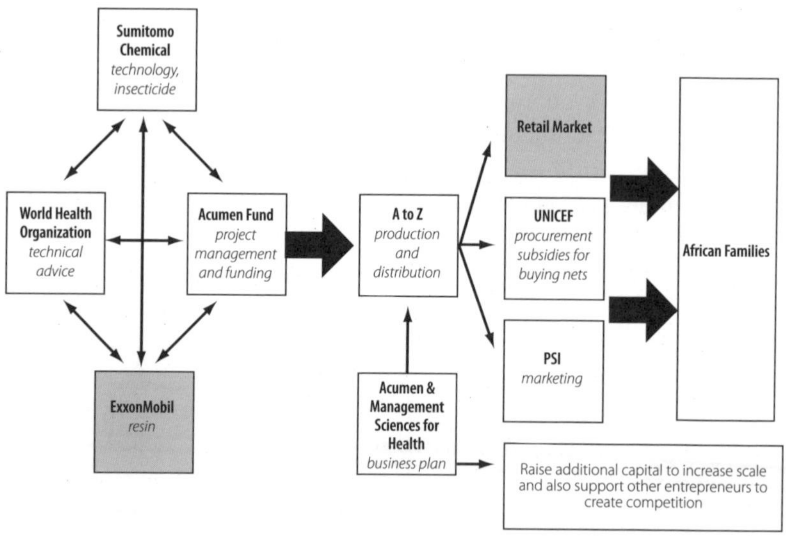

Source: WHO, 2003. "Transfer of Olyset Technology for Scaling up Production of Long-Lasting Insecticidal Nets (LLINs) in Africa" (WHO internal document, 2003).
Note: This diagram represents the original plan for the transfer and does not include the change in ExxonMobil's role described above.

Impact of local production

By 2007, A to Z's annual production capacity had risen to 4 million nets per year. In order to further increase the production capacity, Sumitomo Chemical and A to Z set up a joint venture called Vector Health International, launching production in its Arusha factory in February 2007. Together with this new company, the total production capacity as of

December 2008 expanded to 19 million nets a year. Reports have started to appear showing a marked reduction of malaria infection rates in villages that have received nets donated from A to Z's plant.[8] For example, in one village in Kenya, blood tests conducted two years after the distribution of Olyset nets revealed that the number of people carrying malarial parasites dropped from 50.1 percent of the population to 10.8 percent.[9] As an indirect economic effect, A to Z's overall efficiency in manufacturing the Olyset nets and other products has risen, and it has won recognition as a company with one of the highest levels of productivity in all of Africa. In addition, the company is contributing to the local economy by employing approximately 4,000 people at relatively high salaries. Also, by protecting people from malaria, the Olyset nets keep people healthy, which makes them more productive and saves them precious resources that would otherwise be used on treatment.[10]

On the cost side, meanwhile, local production in Africa has not led to the savings that were initially expected. This has been explained as reflecting the shortcomings in the area of transport infrastructure for the materials, along with the fact that local employee skill levels do not compare favorably with those found in China and Vietnam, which means that total personnel costs are not lower.[11] This suggests that African countries and their development partners need to consider measures to further improve the conditions for local production by transnational companies.

---

8. Global Health Initiative, "Public-Private Partnership Case Example."
9. James O. Waiero, et al., "Bednet Use in the Sauri Millennium Village" (Powerpoint presentation at the annual meeting of the Alliance for Malaria Prevention, Geneva, October 6, 2008). According to Waiero, only 22 percent of households were using bednets in Sauri before distribution began in 2005 as part of the Millennium Village project, but in 2007, Olyset nets were being used by 87.8 percent of households, and of those roughly 90 percent reported using them every day. While this undoubtedly contributed to the reduction in malaria infection in the village, the use of bednets alone was not the sole factor. The village took a comprehensive approach to fighting malaria, including distributing drugs to treat malaria and spraying insecticides to reduce the mosquito population.
10. Acumen Fund, *Investment Report, August 2005*.
11. Interview with Hideo Wada, Sumitomo Chemical.

From Business to Social Investment

Leadership to increase production

The production of Olyset nets has expanded dramatically not just in Africa but throughout Sumitomo Chemical as a whole. From a mere 20,000 in 1999, annual production increased with the addition of the Changzhou plant in China in 2002 and of a new factory built in Arusha (operated by A to Z) in 2003, bringing the total to 5 million nets in 2005. The company has continued to build up its production capacity since then, adding plants in Dalian, China; Ho Chi Minh City, Vietnam; and another in Tanzania (operated by Vector Health). As of December 2008, the total number of nets produced reached 38 million. A new plant is now being considered in Nigeria, with a maximum production capacity of 20 million nets per year. The company is now offering a full range of products to fight malaria, centering on the Olyset net but also including insecticide sprays and larvicides.

When it started to develop the Olyset net, Sumitomo Chemical did not expect it to turn into such a major business. As a manufacturer of pesticide ingredients, it was continuing its efforts to come up with materials to control malaria, but initially the net did not draw much attention within the company. Dr. Itoh, who was involved in the development process for many years, recalls that the turning point in terms of gaining in-house attention came around 2003–2004. At a launching ceremony on the eve of the third Tokyo International Conference on African Development in September 2003, Sumitomo Chemical exhibited the Olyset net in cooperation with UNICEF. In advance of the conference, the two organizations also made a joint press announcement on the free transfer of technology to Tanzania. This was the first major media coverage of the Olyset net. The following year, the groundbreaking ceremony for the new A to Z plant, which the president of Tanzania attended, was widely covered in the media and cited as a good example of public-private partnership, and it was through this attention that the company's executives and people in other departments became familiar with the Olyset net. This recognition has continued to increase and has been bolstered by the international campaign against malaria.

At the World Economic Forum Davos conference in January 2005, Sumitomo Chemical President Hiromasa Yonekura joined Columbia University Professor Jeffrey Sachs and then Global Fund Executive Director Richard Feacham for a press conference at which the development of mosquito nets and the local production in Tanzania were introduced and won high praise. President Yonekura himself noted that he had the sense of having been thrust upon the main stage at the strong request of the United Nations and others involved in the campaign against malaria. It is certainly likely that the fact that the company's cooperation was directly requested at a high level from international organizations like the WHO and UNICEF contributed to the executive decision to increase production of the Olyset nets. Another favorable factor was that international organizations gave clear and concrete indications of demand for the product (with UNICEF initially predicting demand for 20 million nets).

Expansion into the field of philanthropy

Sumitomo Chemical began making philanthropic contributions to the fight against malaria in 2005, in addition to the contribution it was already making through its mosquito net business operations. This move is partially a response to the good business results it has enjoyed in the first few years of the 21st century and partially reflective of the increased talk in Japan about corporate social responsibility.

In March 2005, the company responded favorably to a request from the United Nations Foundation for a donation of ¥44 million (US$370,000) for the Africa Live 2005 Roll Back Malaria Concert, becoming a major sponsor of the event. The concert was broadcast in Africa and Europe, reaching 450 million viewers. In August and December of that year, the company donated a portion of its profits from the Olyset net totaling ¥30 million (US$250,000), to a nongovernmental organization (NGO), World Vision Japan, to provide support for education in Africa. The company has continued to work with this organization to build schools in Africa.

Sumitomo Chemical's philanthropic undertakings expanded in 2006. In March, the company decided to contribute to the Millennium Villages project based at Columbia University's Earth Institute. This project targets especially impoverished African villages as model sites—extending assistance with farming technology, food, education, and healthcare—as part of the drive to eradicate severe poverty, one of the MDGs. Sumitomo Chemical provided 330,000 Olyset nets (worth approximately ¥150 million or US$1.25 million) free of charge to help make the model villages malaria free. Nets were distributed to 100 villages of approximately 5,000 people each, saving approximately 500,000 people from the threat of malaria.

The company has continued to distribute nets, funding, and other goods to countries in Africa and elsewhere in cooperation with the Roll Back Malaria Partnership, UNICEF, and the international NGO Malaria No More, among others.

Sumitomo Chemical has won recognition for its sustained efforts in the areas of product development and philanthropy. In June 2005, the Olyset net was selected by *Time Magazine* as one of the "Coolest Inventions of 2004." In September 2006, the company received the Asahi Corporate Citizen Award from the *Asahi Shimbun*, one of Japan's leading newspapers, and in November of that year it was chosen as a laureate in the health category under the Tech Museum Awards program (operated by the Tech Museum of Innovation in San Jose, California), an international program recognizing innovative uses of technology that bring sustained benefit and contribute to solving the most pressing problems facing humanity.

Originally established for the purpose of removing the noxious sulfur dioxide from the emissions at Sumitomo's Besshi copper mine in Shikoku, Japan, and to use the chemical to manufacture fertilizer, Sumitomo Chemical has become a leading company in the fight against malaria. The company's experience offers useful lessons for other companies looking for ways to develop marketable products that will benefit both the company itself and communities looking for new tools to use in the fight.

Interviews

Dr. Pierre Guillet, Vector Control & Prevention, Global Malaria Programme, WHO (via email)

Dr. Takaaki Itoh, Manager, Marketing Department, International Environmental Health Division, Sumitomo Chemical

Hiroshi Kuroda, Manager, Marketing Department, International Environmental Health Division, Sumitomo Chemical

Katsuyuki Sakai, Manager, General Affairs Department, Sumitomo Chemical

Mio Suzuki, Corporate Communications Department, Sumitomo Chemical

Hideo Wada, Manager, Affiliates & Overseas Project Team, Planning & Coordination Office, Agricultural Chemicals Sector, Sumitomo Chemical

Toyota South Africa Motors
Mainstreaming HIV/AIDS Programming

South Africa is richly endowed with natural mineral resources and plays a leading role in the economic growth of Africa, enjoying high levels of foreign direct investment. The preferential treatment that the government gives to the automobile industry has persuaded many car manufacturers to establish operations in South Africa, including Toyota. Sub-Saharan African countries, however, are also known for their high prevalence of HIV/AIDS. Among them, South Africa is said to have one of the highest rates in the world, with 5.5 million people infected by HIV.[1] For labor-intensive enterprises in the mining and automobile manufacturing industries, the spread of HIV/AIDS among employees is a serious threat to production that even has the potential to lead to business paralysis. As such, many enterprises have introduced measures to deal with HIV/AIDS without awaiting government initiatives. As one of the largest enterprises in South Africa, Toyota South Africa Motors has been implementing a workplace HIV/AIDS program since 1993. While the workplace programs of other countries' automobile makers—such as those of BMW and DaimlerChrysler—are internationally well known, little recognition has been given so far to efforts started more than a decade ago by a Japanese manufacturer in tackling the issue at the local factory level. Because of the low prevalence of HIV/AIDS in Japan, the level of interest demonstrated by Japanese enterprises is considered to be generally low. However, it is important to recognize this pioneering example of an effort that was independently initiated by a Japanese manufacturer at the local level in a country heavily affected by HIV/AIDS.

1. UNAIDS, "Report on the Global AIDS Epidemic" (Geneva: UNAIDS, 2006), 455.

Types of activities related to HIV/AIDS

- Explicit policy of nondiscrimination based on serostatus
- Use of peer educators and other tools to raise awareness about HIV/AIDS in the workplace
- Provision of information on voluntary counseling and testing (VCT) services
- Provision of condoms in company facilities
- Provision of care and treatment for HIV-positive employees
- Support for AIDS orphans in the community

South African production of Toyota cars was initially launched in 1962 by a local car manufacturing company, with Toyota's direct investment starting only in 1996. The headquarters and sales office are located near Johannesburg, and a large-scale factory has been built on the outskirts of Durban. Of the present production of 149,000 cars per year, 70 percent is aimed at the domestic market. The company employs approximately 10,000 salaried and hourly workers, making it one of the largest employers in South Africa.

The high prevalence of HIV/AIDS in South Africa has serious implications for the production line, with the company experiencing a 1 percent attrition rate every year due to health-related conditions. The majority of these deaths and health-related incapacities are believed to be related to HIV/AIDS. The health conditions of the approximately 10 percent of employees predicted to be HIV-positive also threaten to have a negative impact on stable production. Despite the job-related education and training provided to improve production capacity, high rates of absenteeism, early retirement, and death of employees hinder production and lower the general morale. To ensure stable economic activity, wellness activities focusing on HIV/AIDS were implemented in the workplace starting in 1993. Toyota's executive vice president Hiroyuki Niwa stressed that the program "was nothing special, just a natural consequence of what needed to be done by a manufacturer with 10,000 employees in South Africa."

There are several factors that are believed to have triggered the spread of HIV/AIDS in South Africa. Although it is one of the relatively wealthy countries in Africa, the great disparity between rich and poor regions in South Africa has forced many people into migrant work, which has been proven to help fuel the spread of the disease. In particular, male migrant workers who are forced to leave their homes and families to work in mining and general industry in urban and industrial areas tend to visit commercial sex workers, significantly elevating their risk of infection. Another reason may be attributed to the custom of polygamy among some of the tribes. In addition, political factors also came into play. The early detection of the spread of the epidemic coincided with the end of apartheid, and the confusion accompanying the transition to a democratic system did not permit the government to implement appropriate measures to counter the spread. Even in the late 1990s when antiretroviral (ARV) treatment became available, the South African government was reluctant to adopt its use in the public sector, questioning the safety of the medication. It was not until 2004, after much pressure from people living with HIV/AIDS and the international community, that ARV became available at public health and medical institutions. This delay in introducing ARV treatment also added momentum to the spread.

With the government lagging behind in implementing appropriate measures, it was the private sector that offered education, awareness, prevention, treatment, and care to people suffering from HIV/AIDS in South Africa. Private medical institutions are well developed in South Africa and people who could afford to pay for them had access to ARV treatment. On the other hand, those who could not afford the cost and needed to rely on public institutions did not have access to new medications and thus lost their lives. Under such circumstances, some of the major enterprises started to promote HIV testing and offered care to people living with HIV/AIDS as part of their employee welfare programs. As ARV treatment gained international recognition, some enterprises embarked on longer-term commitments to make ARV treatment available. At present, the South African government is said to be targeting its HIV/AIDS measures to the highly vulnerable population suffering under extreme poverty or unemployment, while relying on those in the private sector to take the initiative to cover their own employees.

HIV/AIDS Program at Toyota South Africa Motors

In South Africa, HIV/AIDS is given special legal treatment under such laws as the Labour Relations Act, Employment Equity Act, and Health and Safety Act. Employers are prohibited from discriminating against an employee on the basis of serostatus, and discharging an employee on this basis is illegal. Instead, HIV-positive employees are to be treated the same as any other employees with disabilities or other challenges. The legal system similarly prohibits mandatory HIV testing of employees or job applicants. Within Toyota South Africa Motors, the management and the labor union have an agreement that employees with any disability are allowed to continue working as long as they are able, and HIV infection is covered under this agreement.

Toyota South Africa Motors' HIV/AIDS program was launched in 1993 at the initiative of Harry Gazendam, executive vice president of corporate affairs. The main objective of the program is to put a stop to the spread of HIV/AIDS by preventing new infections. It also aims to offer appropriate treatment and care to those already infected with HIV in order to maintain their health and allow them to continue working. In order to achieve these two objectives, the health team's focus is on education and awareness programs aimed at reducing stigma and creating an atmosphere of openness on the subject of HIV/AIDS in the workplace.

The program is operated by a health team under the supervision of the executive vice president. The team is composed of 10 staff members, including a medical doctor, HIV/AIDS specialists, nurses, and social workers. There is also a person in charge of occupational health for each department. As is explained in greater detail below, the bulk of the activities deal with educating employees about HIV/AIDS, promoting VCT, and offering treatment and care to those employees found to be HIV positive. In the case of sexually transmitted infections, care is extended to include referrals for spouses and children of the infected employees to health facilities in the community, and the program reaches out in other ways to the communities in which the employees live. The cost of the HIV/AIDS program is about 1.3 million rand (approximately US$186,000) per year, not including personnel costs.

HIV/AIDS programs such as Toyota's are conducted by most large corporations operating in South Africa, albeit with varying degrees of coverage and comprehensiveness. They are particularly conspicuous in large-scale mining and automobile industries, Toyota being no exception. However, Toyota's program differs from many in that the HIV/AIDS component is incorporated into the overall health or "wellness" program and is not a stand-alone priority. The company includes an Employee Assistance Program (EAP) in its wellness program to offer services for maintaining the physical and mental health of its employees.[2]

2. The EAP offers professional employment-based health services designed to assist in the identification and resolution of a broad range of employees' personal concerns (e.g., health, marital, family, financial, or emotional problems; substance and alcohol abuse; legal issues; stress; etc.) that may affect job performance. It was

By promoting a comprehensive health program based on EAP principles and mainstreaming HIV/AIDS into its wellness activities, it aims to create an atmosphere of openness on the subject of HIV/AIDS.

The following activities are included in Toyota South Africa Motors' workplace HIV/AIDS program:

HIV/AIDS education program for employees

Posters and pamphlets are placed in various places along the production line and in plant facilities to increase general awareness and give daily alerts about prevention and how to deal with HIV/AIDS once a person tests positive. At the same time, peer educators are selected from among the employees and provided with training in order to enable them to advise employees and refer them to the wellness services. Peer educators are allowed to spend one hour per week to perform their duties during working hours. Originally called "HIV/AIDS peer educators," their name has been changed to "wellness educators" in order to cover a wider spectrum of health issues, including chronic diseases other than HIV/AIDS, general health management, and drug addiction.

Prevention of new infections through VCT

In order to prevent the spread of HIV infection, people must first know their own serostatus. Toyota South Africa Motors encourages its employees and their family members to undergo VCT by providing information on hospitals and other facilities where such testing can be done. Medical personnel within the company are trained to offer VCT services in the company clinic. All such testing is conducted on a voluntary basis and remains completely confidential. Only the doctor has knowledge of the test results, which are not reported to the employer or any member of the management. At present, 11 percent of the employees have been tested, with the percentage on the increase. Efforts are also made to promote the use of condoms, which have yet to gain wide acceptance in society. Condoms are provided in dispensers placed in the company locker rooms and restrooms.

---

originally offered to employees with alcohol dependence in the United States in the 1940s, gradually expanding to cover a wider range of health and other employment-related issues. Of the Fortune 500 companies, 95 percent have incorporated the program in their workplaces.

Treatment and medical services

Trained medical staff provide information on proper nutrition and dietary supplements for HIV-positive employees and family members at the company's expense. As for ARV treatment, the company clinic reached an agreement with the local Department of Health in November 2006 to receive pre-packed ARV drugs free of charge, which the company provides directly to its employees.[3] Monitoring of the health conditions of HIV-infected employees is also essential, and the company performs clinical assessments to determine whether individual employees are able to meet their job expectations. Fair and equitable treatment is to be ensured if they are still able to meet their job requirements. If they become incapable of meeting expectations, transfers and alternative work arrangements are made, or they are given assistance with applications for sick leave and welfare benefits, and recommendations are made for their return to work once it is deemed appropriate.

Community outreach

Most of the employees live near the manufacturing plant in an area inhabited by many impoverished families and known for widespread prevalence of HIV/AIDS. As such, Toyota South Africa Motors partners with local volunteer groups and takes part in various projects and events, such as sending its employees as volunteers to an AIDS orphan center, visiting employees on sick leave, putting up posters, and promoting awareness-raising and educational events on HIV/AIDS. In a country like South Africa, where HIV/AIDS has come to be a major social issue, cooperation and sharing of information beyond the scope of one company is essential. Toyota South Africa Motors plays an active role in the HIV/AIDS committee of the Durban Chamber of Commerce and the South Africa Business Coalition on HIV/AIDS to raise greater awareness of the issue in the South African economic sector.

---

3. ARV treatment, however, is only dispensed to employees and not to their dependants. Counseling, testing, and treatment services are arranged for family members at various community-based centers in Kwazulu-Natal free of charge, and the company advises employees' family members of the availability of such services.

Inclusive participation

The company nurse on the health team emphasizes the importance of encouraging the entire staff to take part in the program in order to ensure that the HIV/AIDS program is effective in the workplace, especially in manufacturing factories. The roles assigned are as follows:[4]

Health Staff	Define objectives and deliver on-site wellness services
Management	Buy-in and support of programs to enable achievement of objectives
	Enable employees to participate in company HIV/AIDS program
	Support employees returning to work, including support for task reallocation as necessary
	Refer employees unable to meet performance, behavior, and attendance targets to Toyota Wellness Services
Union[5]	Support and encourage members to participate in the program
	Refer employees to Wellness Services
	Provide suggestions on how to improve program effectiveness
Wellness/Peer Educators	Promote VCT
	Create awareness of the wellness, EAP, and HIV/AIDS programs
	Participate in company HIV/AIDS and wellness activities
	Participate in community outreach activities such as offering help to people living with HIV/AIDS and to AIDS orphans
All Employees	Make use of the program

4. Sr. Sma Madonda, Toyota South Africa Health Team, "Toyota SA Wellness Activities: Onsite HIV/AIDS Program and Community Support" (Powerpoint presentation, 2006).
5. Labor unions have traditionally been strong in South Africa and they are often in confrontation with management. However, according to Executive Vice President Harry Gazendam of Toyota South Africa Motors, there has been little disagreement between the union and the management on the issue of HIV/AIDS. It is one of the rare areas in which the two sides are cooperating in the joint interest of maintaining the health of all employees.

Achievements of the Toyota South Africa Motors Program

Impact

The impact of the program can be determined from statistics gathered in several areas. For instance, a total of 207 peer educators have been trained since 2002 and their activities are becoming more and more prominent in the workplace. As awareness of the wellness and EAP programs has grown, the number of employees who have sought out services under these programs has soared from 377 in 2004 to 455 in 2005, and to 647 in 2006. Some of that increase can be attributed to the VCT program, as 11 percent of the staff have voluntarily presented themselves for VCT. A steady increase per annum has been noted for on-site tests performed at Toyota Health Services, starting with 140 in 2003, 211 in 2004, 338 in 2005, and 397 in 2006. These figures do not include employees on medical aid who have elected to go for VCT at private doctors' offices, hospitals, or community clinics. Thus, an even larger number of employees are believed to have taken HIV tests.

One positive byproduct of Toyota's HIV/AIDS program in South Africa is the relationships that the company has been able to build and strengthen with outside agencies and community-based organizations. The work that Toyota is doing to support vulnerable populations has helped the company to become more integrated into the communities where it operates, which has a positive impact on its public image in South Africa.

Finally, while it is still too early in the program to determine the overall health impact of the program in terms of the number of new HIV infections or deaths caused by AIDS, the health team's analysis indicates that applications for medical disability are reflecting a downward trend. There are likely other factors at play in this trend as well, but it seems to indicate that programs such as the one at Toyota are making a contribution by raising awareness and reducing stigma.

Corporate impact

The contribution of this HIV/AIDS workplace program has been recognized by the Employee Assistance Professionals Association, which actively deals with issues of HIV/AIDS in the workplace and which gave an award to Mr. Dawie Spohr, senior specialist in Toyota South Africa Motors' health services, for his dedication over many years. The program also gathered attention in Japan when it was covered in a news program by NHK (Japan's public television network). It was also introduced in Toyota headquarters' 2005 corporate social responsibility report under a section on the promotion of safety and health. For Toyota South Africa Motors, the program is operated purely in the interest of ensuring a healthy workforce and not for social recognition.[6] However, it cannot be denied that the program offers an exemplary case of a leading Japanese enterprise developing professional health staff within the company and offering much-needed health services to its employees and the community in which they live and work.

Interviews

Hiroyuki Niwa, Executive Vice President and Chief Coordinating Executive, Toyota South Africa Motors

Harry Gazendam, Executive Vice President, Corporate Affairs, Toyota South Africa Motors

Yoshimitsu Morita, Senior Vice President, Manufacturing, Toyota South Africa Motors

Masaru Adachi, Vice President, Human Resources, Toyota South Africa Motors

M. Minty, General Manager, Group Health Services, Toyota South Africa Motors

Dawie Spohr, Senior Specialist, Group Health Services, Toyota South Africa Motors

Sr. Sma Madonda, Chronic Diseases Coordinator, Toyota South Africa Motors

6. Quoted from an interview with Executive Vice President Harry Gazendam of Toyota South Africa.

Bayer China

Empowering the Media to Save Lives

An estimated 700,000 people in China are infected with HIV, creating some of the world's most serious anxiety about the spread of this disease.[1] Considering China's immense population, a more rapid spread of infection in China would contribute to further large-scale spread throughout the rest of East Asia and the world. Therefore, an effective response to AIDS in China is in everyone's interest.

Bayer is a Germany-based global pharmaceutical and healthcare company. It is involved around the world in promoting health through its business activities—research, development, and marketing of pharmaceuticals—as well as through its corporate social responsibility.

China represents Bayer's second largest market in Asia, and the company is playing a leading role in the fight against HIV/AIDS there. Among its activities in this area, the most unique is a partnership with a university research institute that aims to strengthen news media and information dissemination on HIV/AIDS. Using the company's core competency in health-related communications, it is a good example of a pioneering effort to fight the spread of HIV/AIDS from a variety of angles.

Types of activities related to HIV/AIDS

- Raising awareness of HIV/AIDS and reducing stigma and discrimination against people living with HIV/AIDS through the media
- Supporting AIDS orphans through a partnership with a university and government agencies
- Raising awareness of HIV/AIDS prevention in the workplace
- Strengthening news reporting and information dissemination on HIV/AIDS through a partnership with a university

1. UNAIDS, "Focus of China's AIDS Response," September 18, 2008, www.unaids.org/en/KnowledgeCentre/Resources/FeatureStories/archive/2008/20080918_Focus_on_China_AIDS_response.asp.

HIV/AIDS in China

The initial outbreak of HIV/AIDS in China occurred among injecting drug users along the area adjacent to the Golden Triangle—known for its illicit manufacturing and trafficking of drugs—and among commercial plasma donors in poor rural areas. Subsequently, infection began spreading more through sexual contact, particularly among commercial sex workers in large urban areas, gradually expanding to the general public. Now, the main transmission routes are through sexual contact and injecting drug use with contaminated needles and syringes. China now has the fastest-growing AIDS epidemic in the world, and in 2007 alone, an estimated 50,000 people were newly infected with HIV in China.[2]

The first case of AIDS in China was diagnosed in 1985, but the country did not have adequate laws and policies to deal with the disease effectively. The Chinese government did not show an active commitment to fighting HIV/AIDS until after the 2003 SARS outbreak heightened awareness of the importance of public health. Still, the public's knowledge of the threat posed by HIV/AIDS and how it can be prevented remains alarmingly limited. In February 2004, China established a State Council Working Committee on HIV/AIDS, and its working committee developed a national policy framework for HIV/AIDS the next month, which eventually led to the enactment in 2006 of China's HIV/AIDS Act—the first of its kind in China to specify a particular disease. As the government has begun to engage in cross-sectoral efforts to address HIV/AIDS, it has appealed to the business sector for its cooperation.

Bayer China's Approach to HIV/AIDS

Bayer began doing business in China in 1882, and today China represents the company's second largest market in Asia. Bayer China is among the most prominent foreign companies in China, with 19 groups and 4,900 employees in the country and annual revenues totaling more than €1.26 billion (US$1.63 billion). Bayer China has also been playing an active role in corporate social responsibility in China. People often think that Bayer would have a natural interest in engaging in the fight against HIV/AIDS

2. State Council AIDS Working Committee Office and UN Theme Group on AIDS, *UNGASS Country Progress Report*, 2008, data.unaids.org/pub/Report/2008/china_2008_country_progress_report_en.pdf.

simply because it is a pharmaceutical company. But Bayer does not, in fact, manufacture any drugs for HIV/AIDS. It does have a natural interest in public health more broadly, though, and as a global corporation, it also possesses core competency in health-related communications. This situation and the sheer magnitude of the challenge of HIV/AIDS in China led Bayer to place AIDS-related activities at the core of its social activities in China.

The Global Business Coalition on HIV/AIDS (GBC) launched an office in China in 2004 to mobilize corporate support for HIV/AIDS and other major communicable diseases. Most of GBC China's approximately 60 member companies are foreign companies, but there has been a gradual increase in local Chinese members, with eight companies now claiming membership. Bayer China was one of the original members of GBC China, and the company's general manager for corporate communications, William Valentino, heads the GBC China AIDS Working Group. In that role, Bayer China has pioneered the way in encouraging corporate participation in the response to AIDS in China and is one of the most active corporations in this area.

Bayer China's various AIDS-related activities include support for the Positive Art Workshop, which aims to reduce stigma and discrimination by nurturing artistic skills of people living with HIV/AIDS; projects helping AIDS orphans; and the provision of HIV prevention education to employees and their families. But perhaps its key contribution has been in the media field.

Given the low level of awareness about HIV/AIDS, how it is spread, and how it can be prevented, the media has an urgent role to play in educating the general public. According to a recent survey conducted in six major cities in China, many people lack basic knowledge of how HIV infection is transmitted. Of the people surveyed, 48.7 percent believed that HIV could be spread through mosquito bites, and 18.3 percent believed it could be spread by coughing or sneezing. Alarmingly, 43.1 percent of the respondents had never used a condom and 88.1 percent believed themselves immune to such infection. The survey also indicated that those with lower awareness and understanding of HIV/AIDS had greater discriminatory opinions of the disease.[3] Clearly, it would be impossible to stem the spread of HIV in China without raising people's awareness of how the virus is spread and changing their attitudes and behavior regarding safe sex.

3. China AIDS Media Partnership (CHAMP), *AIDS-Related Knowledge, Attitudes, Behavior, and Practices: A Survey of 6 Chinese Cities* (China: CHAMP, 2008), 10–11.

According to the former executive director of the Joint United Nations Programme on HIV/AIDS, Peter Piot, "The media has the unparalleled ability to save millions of lives by providing them with vital life-saving information on AIDS and creating a supporting environment for social change."[4] Or, as Valentino explains it, people go to the doctor when they are sick, but that is not where they learn how to prevent infection, so in a sense, the media has the potential to save more lives through prevention education than doctors can through treatment. Valentino recognized that the role that communications could play in HIV prevention, care, and support was underestimated and underutilized in China, and he identified the better use of behavior change through communications strategies as a critical factor in breaking the silence about HIV/AIDS. These strategies could push the topic into the public sphere, the only place where the spread of infection could be controlled.

In 2004, the company launched a comprehensive approach to HIV/AIDS by establishing the "Tsinghua-Bayer Public Health and HIV/AIDS Media Studies Program." Recognizing that the media have an important role to play in eliminating the stigma and discrimination that surround HIV/AIDS, it established this program to strengthen news media reporting and information sharing on HIV/AIDS and other public health and healthcare challenges. The program seeks to establish a national platform for high-quality, conscientious healthcare reporting by engaging and training media professionals. The ultimate objective is to promote the development of leaders and experts dedicated to responsible reporting on HIV/AIDS, other chronic diseases, and healthcare-related issues in China. Specific activities are organized into three clusters:

Media research
Applied research is undertaken to track and monitor the coverage of HIV/AIDS in China's mainstream media as well as in foreign media, accompanied by analysis on the strengths and weaknesses of Chinese media coverage. Research results are published as academic papers and used to encourage more academic research on HIV/AIDS reporting.

Media advocacy
Workshops on HIV/AIDS and other healthcare issues are held for people working in television, magazines, and newspapers. The aim of

4. Kaiser Family Foundation, "United Nations-Supported Global Media AIDS Initiative Announces New Media Efforts to Address HIV/AIDS in Russia, India, China, Indonesia and U.S.," July 13, 2004, www.kff.org/entpartnerships/phip071304-nr.cfm.

this component is to create a foundation for high-quality reporting by creating forums for dialogue among people in the media, sharing opinions and experiences, and exchanging information.

Journalist training
Through regular workshops, journalists and other media professionals from around China are brought together in an attempt to develop human resources with expertise on HIV/AIDS and other healthcare issues.

This program is a collaborative effort among the International Communications Department of the Tsinghua University School of Journalism, Bayer China, the Ministry of Health, the Ministry of Science and Technology, the central government's Publicity Department, the State Council's Information Office, and media professionals in China and abroad. In addition to its role in creating the program, in 2004 Bayer China contributed US$36,200 to the program, and from 2005 to 2007 it continued its contribution at US$32,600 per year.

Impact

The research results and activities of this project are made public on the Internet and used by governmental and international agencies, thereby making a strong contribution to the improvement of the quality and quantity of news reporting and information available on HIV/AIDS in China. More than 1,000 media professionals have been trained by this program in more than 20 workshops all over China. Of those, 40 also took part in a training session for journalists during the 16th International AIDS Conference in Toronto, Canada, in 2006, allowing them to experience the connection between HIV/AIDS and the media in an international setting as well. In an attempt to encourage the media to take more responsibility for reporting on HIV/AIDS, Bayer China and Tsinghua University established the Tsinghua-Bayer Media Award for Responsible Public Health Coverage in 2006. The two partners plan to expand their information-dissemination program to address a wide variety of public health issues and will begin addressing additional communicable and chronic diseases such as diabetes, cardiovascular disease, hypertension, tuberculosis, and hepatitis.

By supporting this program, Bayer China acknowledges that corporate activity must extend beyond the horizons of the local business context and community to build partnerships with other stakeholders. Bayer China views this program as a demonstration of its deep-rooted commitment to corporate social responsibility, assuming broader responsibilities to society and serving a wider range of human values.

Bayer China hopes to continue to expand its program in order to increase awareness of transmission, prevention, care, and treatment of HIV/AIDS; reduce stigma and discrimination against people with HIV/AIDS; stem the spread of HIV infection through behavioral and attitudinal change; improve access to and quality of treatment; and contribute to the overall fight against the epidemic. In addition, if the company is going to play a role in the global fight against AIDS, leaders in company headquarters will need to be convinced of the value of the program in China and the potential value of expanding its principles to Bayer's operations around the world.

Access to accurate information on HIV/AIDS is a critical element in fighting this epidemic. Bayer China has been a pioneer by bringing attention to the significant role of the news media in this battle and by using its core competency as a healthcare specialist to promote information sharing on issues related to HIV/AIDS and public health.

Central Azucarera Don Pedro
Local Partnership for Better Health

According to the World Health Organization (WHO), 9.2 million people were afflicted with tuberculosis (TB) in 2007 and some 1.8 million died of the disease worldwide.[1] The vast majority of TB patients live in developing countries, and most of those afflicted are in the productive years of 15–54. This fact alone points to the significant compounded social burden of TB in communities least equipped to deal with the challenge. As the number of patients co-infected with TB and HIV increases, it is now feared that the continuing worldwide spread of HIV will spark even greater increases in the incidence of TB.

The Philippines is no exception to these trends, being among the highest TB-burdened countries in the world. Central Azucarera Don Pedro (CADPI), a major Filipino sugar manufacturer located a couple of hours from Manila on Luzon—the largest island in the Philippines and by far the most populous—is trying to deal with this challenge by implementing a comprehensive workplace TB control program. In addition to its workplace program, CADPI provides prevention education and medical treatment to the local community in partnership with local health centers and other public organizations. This is a pioneering example in which a local company in an Asian developing country is tackling a global problem using its corporate resources.

Types of activities related to tuberculosis:

- Workplace guidelines against discrimination based on TB infection
- Workplace education and awareness-raising campaign
- Diagnosis and treatment of TB in company clinic for all employees, employees' family members, and other members of the community

1. World Health Organization (WHO), *Global Tuberculosis Control: Surveillance Planning, Financing* (WHO: Geneva, 2008), 7.

- Expansion of prevention, diagnosis, and treatment services to the local community

Corporate Participation in TB Control

As TB continues to rank as a major cause of death in developing countries—exhibiting signs of reemergence even in industrialized countries—the WHO revised its conventional approach to TB in 1994, introducing what it described as the most efficient and effective intervention package for TB control: the directly observed treatment, short course (DOTS) strategy. The DOTS strategy is a comprehensive set of TB control measures, designed as a short-term, effective treatment to be completed in six to eight months through the use of antitubercular agents, patient engagement, and active monitoring of patient compliance.

In the Philippines, the DOTS strategy has been introduced within the framework of the New National TB Control Project, which began in 1996, and has shown some favorable results. However, the country still has the eighth-highest incidence of TB in the world, with an average of 68 people dying of the disease every day.[2] In rural areas, detection rates are particularly low due to the deep-rooted stigma attached to the disease, and access to proper treatment is difficult. Under these circumstances, increasing treatment ratios is not easy.

In response to these circumstances, the US Agency for International Development (USAID) has supported the dissemination and improvement of the DOTS strategy since 2000 in Metro Manila and five other areas in the Philippines in which better TB-control measures are particularly urgent. In 2002, USAID launched the Philippine Tuberculosis Initiative for the Private Sector, or Philippine TIPS, in an effort to improve TB-control programs in the private sector, including private hospitals, pharmacies, business, and media, as well as through public medical and healthcare organizations. As part of this initiative, the Ministry of Health created a consortium in cooperation with universities, foundations, and the Philippine Coalition Against Tuberculosis as one way to further promote the work of Philippine TIPS. Efforts to disseminate the DOTS strategy in workplaces and in surrounding areas through the use of corporate resources were led by the Philippine Business for Social Progress (PBSP), a member of the

2. Philippine Business for Social Progress. *Pamphlet on DOTS in the Workplace.*

consortium, and a corporate-led social development foundation with a strong network in both the business and civil society sectors.

At the outset of the initiative, the PBSP proposed three models for corporate participation, taking into account the extent and size of business operations, the level of corporate commitment by the management class, and the availability of a health infrastructure in the community. The first model aimed to have large-scale companies that possess their own clinic and testing facilities provide comprehensive TB services to their employees, their employees' dependents, walk-in clients, and other community members who are not directly employed by or otherwise connected to the company. The second was to have companies that do not have their own medical facilities promote medical check-ups among their employees and refer anyone suspected of having TB to the local public health facility, creating a kind of public-private cooperation to ensure complete recovery of individuals and thereby healthier communities. The third model was to establish a private-private partnership scheme in areas where there are no public healthcare centers and refer patients believed to have TB to a private health maintenance organization for treatment. CADPI was selected as a company to pilot the first model, through which it has extended coverage beyond the workplace to members of employees' households, informal workers and service providers, the immediate community, and a wider "adopted" community.[3]

TB-Control Program at CADPI

Efforts in the workplace

CADPI has its headquarters and sugar manufacturing plant in Nasugbu, Batangas, on the west coast of Luzon, approximately 100 kilometers from Manila. The company is a wholly owned subsidiary of the CADPI Group Corporation and one of the largest sugar corporations in the country, handling 11,000 tons of sugar cane daily with an output of 18,000 bags per day. The company plays an important role in the city, leading the social and economic development of the community. It employs about 800 workers, mainly as laborers at the factory, but it also engages with several thousand informal employees and other stakeholders in and around the province of Batangas, including sugar cane farmers, seasonal

3. The other two companies were Toyota Motor Philippines and American Standard, a bath and kitchen product manufacturer.

workers at the farms, truck drivers, suppliers, and retailers. The area is among those known for having a high TB infection rate, with TB being a common affliction among employees and their families. The company is thus very aware of the necessity for TB-control measures.

The first step the company took to initiate the program was to establish an internal structure for the program. It developed comprehensive TB-control guidelines, specifying procedures for testing and treating employees at an in-house clinic and guaranteeing TB patients the right to work without discrimination based on their TB infection status. The company strongly encourages early detection and treatment, in part by guaranteeing that workers infected with TB may continue to work as long as they are under the proper treatment regimen and that any employees who have to temporarily change their duties due to TB-related illness will be allowed to return to their former positions once they are completely cured.

Second, the company established an internal system for implementing the program. CADPI runs an in-house clinic with 20 beds and 21 staff within its factory compound. The facility is open to employees and their family members for health check-ups, as well as to other patients from the community. The company has trained industrial physicians, nurses, and public health aides to implement a comprehensive DOTS strategy centering on the in-house clinic. In addition, divisional and departmental managers have received training in TB control in order to establish a system to promote understanding and collaboration among top management. The Personnel Department is responsible for looking after whether the TB-control measures are in accordance with the guidelines. The department also administers various welfare and personnel matters, such as providing medical bill subsidies and coordinating absences and employees' return to work. A special technical working group has been established under the supervision of the medical director in the Community Development Office to promote preventive education activities for employees and community residents.

At present, CADPI's program includes two pillars: (1) diagnosis and treatment and (2) preventive education. Under the former, sputum smear microscopy tests and X-ray examinations are conducted at the in-house clinic for employees and their families. For each patient found to have TB, a DOTS regimen is started, offered free of charge, until it can be confirmed that the patient is completely cured. A member of the patient's family is responsible for monitoring drug intake in the initial stages, and adherence is later monitored by the clinic nurses when the employee returns to the work place. The technical working group in the Community Development Office, comprised of social workers, undertakes preventive education programs for employees, involving such teaching methods as games and a jingle-writing contest, among others. The team also conducts regular personalized counseling services. Both programs are conducted in close cooperation with the health bureaus of Batangas Province and the PBSP. The cost of TB-control measures in the workplace is approximately US$7,100 annually.

Expansion to the broader community

Since 2004, the company has expanded its workplace TB-control program to six administrative districts in Nasugbu, covering a population of approximately 27,000. Many CADPI employees and their families reside in the city, giving the company both strong roots in the community and a clear incentive to ensure the health of that broader community, since it represents the environment to which CADPI employees are exposed on a daily basis. As it had already been making social contributions through the Roxas Gargollo Foundation, it was only natural that it would expand its TB-control program for employees to include local residents. Prior to implementing its TB-control efforts, the company was already actively involved in family planning, child health services, HIV/AIDS-prevention education campaigns, and other healthcare projects. The network it had formed with the local community through these activities served as a valuable asset in the TB-control program.

Led by the Roxas Gargollo Foundation and CADPI's Community Development Office, the program promotes the following activities, in collaboration with the councils of six community organizations (composed of cooperative and people's organizations) and local health centers.

Prevention education
The health center of each administrative district holds meetings with medical practitioners and local residents. Efforts are also made to develop educational materials for TB control.

Technical assistance
To implement the DOTS strategy in local medical institutions, groups of industrial physicians, public health aides, and a technical working group within the company provide training and instruction for public

health aides at local health centers and for volunteers involved in monitoring daily patient dosages.

Case management and access to medical treatment
If an employee is determined at the in-house clinic to have TB, CADPI refers the employee to the local health center to ensure that the patient will have proper access to treatment.

Establishment of a TB Diagnostic Committee
CADPI facilitated the establishment of a TB Diagnostic Committee (TBDC) through advocacy with the Western Batangas Medical Society. The TBDC serves the needs of a catchment area of approximately 104,000 people. It has improved the overall environment for communities to become involved in fighting TB and has enhanced the capability of local medical institutions to better diagnose and treat TB patients.

It should also be noted that top management at CADPI have taken the initiative to make TB-control activities for the community a core element of the company's corporate social responsibility strategy. Furthermore, the active participation of top management in dealing with global challenges has also contributed to the success of the program. In 2004, for example, at the initiative of the PBSP and others, a Business and Millennium Development Goal (MDG) CEO Advisory Committee was formed to promote progress on the MDGs, which includes the reduction of the TB rate among its various goals. Mr. Pedro E. Roxas, chairman of the CADPI Group, serves as the lead convener of the committee.

Impact

The introduction of the TB control program in the workplace has increased the detection rate among employees to as high as 77.5 percent.[4] The number of employees receiving treatment has also doubled.

The impact is also felt in the community. Among the 42 administrative districts in the Province of Batangas, the 6 in which the program is implemented account for 20 percent of the total TB detected in the entire province. The program has significantly contributed to the prevention of TB in the region. As a result, three more districts have recently been

4. The detection rate targeted by the WHO under the DOTS strategy is 70 percent.

added to the program. In the future, the program will cover all 42 districts, with the aim of making Batangas a "TB-free province."

One major reason for the increased detection rate is that informal workers and others in the community feel more comfortable getting tested for TB now. In the past, many of those who were exhibiting symptoms of TB were afraid to be tested because of the stigma attached to TB. But because of the education efforts and the fact that they know they can get treatment, more people are taking the initiative to get tested. Those who do test positive can return to work two weeks after they begin treatment, whereas in the past they had to take six months off. The shorter period of medical leave is beneficial both for the employees, who need to make a living, and for CADPI itself, which needs to have a stable workforce.

Due to the success at CADPI, 23 companies, with a total of 52,000 employees, are now participating in Philippine TIPS. Of those, 10 are promoting the DOTS strategy not only in the workplace but also in the local communities (as in the case of CADPI), making use of corporate resources and collaborative partnerships to promote TB-control measures. The factors contributing to the success of CADPI include the effective interaction between top management initiatives (with elements of a top-down approach) and identified rank-and-file needs (a bottom-up approach). Company management has actively tackled the TB-control issue, as exemplified by its vocal efforts to encourage broad corporate participation in TB control. Since the outset, the TB-control program has been led by the Community Development Office and the Roxas Gargollo Foundation, both of which have close links with the local community. Through this arrangement, a network that includes the local community has been developed, with the local context and needs properly identified and reflected in the program. Both the top-down and bottom-up approaches have significantly contributed to the effective implementation of the program.

Interviews

Eric E. Camacho, Program Manager, PBSP

Ma. Nilda U. Loresto, Program Officer, Training and Consulting Group, PBSP

Rowena B. Sugay, Research & Material Development Manager, Training and Consulting Group, PBSP

Rosauro Luntayao, Manager, Community Development Group, CADPI

Olivia Carmen P. Ermita, Municipal Health Officer, Nasugbu Health Department

Maria Teresa Angsioca, Public Health Nurse, Wawa Barangay, Nasugbu

Standard Chartered Bank
Championing the Fight against AIDS in the Workplace and the Community

Standard Chartered Bank, headquartered in London, has a unique global footprint. It is comprised of two British banks founded in the mid-1800s, the Standard Bank in South Africa and the Chartered Bank, established in Mumbai and Shanghai with the grant of a Royal Charter by Queen Victoria. The two banks played a key role in expanding trade between Europe and countries in Africa and Asia, and they merged in 1969 to create the Standard Chartered Bank.

As of 2005, the bank employed 75,000 people in more than 1,750 locations serving 70 countries and territories across the Asia Pacific region, South Asia, the Middle East, Africa, the United Kingdom, and the Americas. It is one of the world's most international banks, with employees representing 115 nationalities. Standard Chartered Bank in Thailand—the focus of this case study—employed roughly 2,500 people as of 2006, when the research was conducted for this study. The bank's pre-tax operating profit in 2005 was US$2.681 billion.

Standard Chartered Bank has long been at the forefront of corporate social responsibility, carefully analyzing and managing the potential environmental and social impacts of its major infrastructure projects. It has also worked hard to ensure that people of all nationalities, socioeconomic classes, and physical abilities have access to banking services. The bank encourages its employees to get involved in the social issues on which the bank itself has placed priority: (1) eliminating avoidable blindness and helping people with vision impairments to live full lives, and (2) helping to prevent the spread of HIV/AIDS and supporting people who are infected with and affected by the virus. All employees of the bank are allowed two additional days of paid leave every year to volunteer in one of these areas.

Types of activities related to HIV/AIDS

- Workplace policy
- Employee training through the use of "HIV champions" as peer educators
- Education and awareness messages in the workplace
- Training programs in communities
- Awareness raising through automated teller machines (ATMs)
- Training-of-trainer sessions for corporate clients
- Charity fundraising
- Provision of free testing
- Press and photo releases
- Technical assistance to the Global Fund to Fight AIDS, Tuberculosis and Malaria (the Global Fund)

The Joint United Nations Programme on HIV/AIDS estimates that there are roughly 610,000 people in Thailand infected with HIV, with an adult prevalence rate of approximately 1.4 percent.[1] Because commercial sex work has been one major route of HIV transmission in Thailand, the Thai government ran a successful campaign in the 1990s to require all commercial sex workers in established institutions to use condoms with all of their clients. The campaign played a vital role in helping to slow down the spread of infection in Thailand, but rates are continuing to rise among injecting drug users, who in turn spread the disease to the general population through sexual contact. In addition, there have been a rising number of commercial sex workers who are not working through established institutions, and the authorities are not able to reach them through the "100 Percent Condom Program."

Standard Chartered Bank's activities grew out of four commitments: (1) to create antidiscrimination policies, (2) to provide information and treatment to employees, (3) to raise awareness about HIV prevention within the bank, and (4) to share information outside of the bank. The workplace policy renounces mandatory testing and discrimination, provides for education on HIV/AIDS and how it can be prevented, and ensures access to voluntary counseling and testing, as well as care and treatment services for HIV-positive employees and their dependents.

---

1. UNAIDS, WHO, and UNICEF. "Epidemiological Fact Sheets on HIV and AIDS: 2008 Update, Thailand," apps.who.int/globalatlas/predefinedReports/EFS2008/full/EFS2008_TH.pdf.

In 2003, Standard Chartered Bank trained all of its 30,000 employees in preventing HIV infection and reducing stigma. Since then, it has provided HIV training to all of its new inductees during the orientation program. Roughly two and a half to three hours of the three-day orientation program are dedicated to training on HIV. The trainers in Bangkok have found that, although new employees often question the relevance of such training before the session, they generally understand its value for bankers after they take part in it and give the session high ratings. The training is reinforced with e-mail messages and posters in the office about HIV prevention and stigma.

The trainers attempt to keep participants in the sessions interested by relying primarily on hands-on exercises that illustrate to the participants the ways in which HIV infection is transmitted, the stereotypes that many of us have regarding infection, and the fact that they can continue to interact daily with HIV-positive friends, family members, and coworkers. The program was launched in Africa in 1999 under the title "Staying Alive," and it was rolled out to all countries in the Standard Chartered Group network in 2003, coinciding with the bank's 150th anniversary, under the title "Living with HIV." By changing the title, the bank wanted to illustrate that people infected with HIV are not concerned simply with staying alive but with living healthy, productive lives.

Most of Standard Chartered Bank's branches are in developing countries—concentrated in Africa, Asia, and the Middle East—where the vast majority of HIV infection takes place. As a result, the bank has found that it is important not only to provide its own employees with education on how to protect themselves from infection—as well as how to work productively and comfortably with HIV-positive colleagues—but also to provide such training to members of the communities where it operates, in essence the communities that make up the bank's primary markets. From among its employees, the bank recruits HIV champions who, among other things, go into target communities to provide training.

In Thailand, the HIV champions who offer training in the communities found that their community training sessions included participants from government health agencies and healthcare facilities. They were initially unsure of what they, as bank employees, could offer to such participants who doubtless had more direct experience with HIV in their own professions. But they quickly discovered that their hands-on training program using easy-to-understand terminology resonated even with these and other participants who had undergone training that was much more formal and scientific in nature. They were surprised at the level of engagement, particularly in the question and answer periods.

Many of the training sessions conducted by Standard Chartered Bank staff include a component to bring HIV-positive people in to talk about their own experience living with the virus. The rationale behind that approach is to help reduce stigma by showing participants that people infected with HIV do not necessarily look any different from those who are not infected. It also gives the participants an opportunity to learn firsthand what kinds of challenges a person living with HIV faces, how they monitor their own health, and how they undergo treatment in order to keep themselves healthy and productive. This component helps to break down the barrier between sero-positive and sero-negative people, illustrating that they can work together, learn from each other, and interact on a daily basis without consideration of their HIV status. In some instances, trainers have found the experience to be empowering for the HIV-positive co-trainers, offering them the opportunity to have their voices heard and not have to be afraid of revealing their status. One Standard Chartered Bank executive in Bangkok commented that the program would truly be successful when employees could stand up and say out loud "I am HIV positive, and I work for Standard Chartered Bank."

Another way Standard Chartered Bank reaches out to the community in Thailand is through its ATMs, which offer a powerful, wide-reaching outreach tool. It is using the ATMs to spread messages about HIV prevention and testing with screens that encourage users to have a confidential HIV test.

In 2004, Standard Chartered Bank decided to leverage its relationships with its corporate clients in order to spread awareness of HIV/AIDS and the important role that corporations can play in preventing an even wider spread of infection. Corporate clients have the option of sending one or two representatives to attend free train-the-trainer sessions, where they learn Standard Chartered Bank's approach to training on HIV/AIDS so that they can provide similar training sessions to their own staff and communities. In Thailand, approximately 25,000 people had taken part in the train-the-trainer sessions by the end of 2008, most of them from human resources departments. As the participants in these sessions have gone back to their own companies and communities and trained their colleagues and neighbors, the bank estimates that about 400,000 people have been reached, directly or indirectly, by these sessions.

Standard Chartered Bank HIV champions in Thailand have organized charity fundraisers to raise funds for the Wat Phra Baht Nam Phu temple's

AIDS hospice in Lopburi Province. Despite multiple campaigns to raise awareness about HIV/AIDS, the stigma attached to HIV infection is still very high in Thailand, and there are many people who are disowned by their families when it is revealed that they are HIV positive. Some of them are taken in by temples, which originally began bringing AIDS patients into a kind of hospice so that they could spend their last days in comfort. Ironically, as treatment is prolonging the lives of AIDS patients, the temples are becoming more crowded and are having difficulty supporting all of the people who come to them. Standard Chartered Bank staff in Bangkok decided to raise funds throughout the company for one such temple and found an overwhelming response from their colleagues. In the end, they were able to raise almost 500,000 baht (approximately US$12,500) for the temple.

Employees of Standard Chartered Bank in Thailand found a way to creatively highlight HIV/AIDS during the June 9, 2006, celebrations of the 60th anniversary of the king's ascension to the throne, one of Thailand's most important recent holidays. They teamed up with the Thai Red Cross AIDS Research Centre to offer 2,120 free HIV tests to people who came in pairs to be tested, encouraging people to know their own status. In order to raise awareness beyond the people who took advantage of the free tests, the bank held a press event to talk about the importance of testing. It continues to hold press events and write articles about HIV/AIDS whenever possible to raise general awareness. In one such event, several CEOs from Standard Chartered Bank branches from around the world posed for a picture that ran with a caption saying that they all knew their HIV status. The goal was to convey the message that it is important for everyone to know his or her own status.

Finally, Standard Chartered Bank as a whole is using its financial management skills to assist the Global Fund. In an attempt to make the Global Fund's grants more efficient and effective, it offers financial and management advice to the fund's grant recipients. In one extreme case, in the Gambia, the bank took over the role of coordinating among the various Global Fund recipients.

The Champions

One theme that is found throughout many of the cases in this study is the idea of champions. In some cases, they are celebrities who champion the cause to raise general awareness; in others, they are CEOs who have not only made a personal and professional commitment to fighting the spread of communicable diseases but have also leveraged their own commitments to convince their peers to make similar commitments in their own companies. In Standard Chartered Bank's case, the term "champions" is used for the individual employees—spread out in various departments throughout all of the bank's offices around the world—who volunteer to champion the cause of fighting HIV/AIDS. The bank made a conscious decision to spread the champions throughout the bank rather than having one department implement HIV/AIDS-related activities, creating a broader sense of ownership over the initiatives. As of 2008, there were 850 HIV champions across Standard Chartered Bank's global reach.

The HIV champions are responsible for providing information in the workplace on HIV prevention, treatment, and stigma. They are also the ones who are responsible for providing training sessions for new employees and for their communities, as well as for organizing fund-raising and volunteer events with their coworkers. In Southeast Asia, an initial group of champions was trained in Malaysia and then tasked with recruiting and training other champions when they returned to their workplaces.

The champions within Standard Chartered Bank were not hired to work on HIV/AIDS-related activities or even on social issues more broadly. They were all hired as regular bank employees and are expected first and foremost to perform effectively in that role. As volunteers, their work on HIV/AIDS is something that each individual champion makes a personal commitment to doing above and beyond their normal bank duties. They are encouraged, however, by the bank leadership to take their HIV/AIDS-related work as seriously as they do their other work. It is standard practice for all Standard Chartered Bank employees to set job objectives for their work. The champions and others who are working on HIV/AIDS include their social activities in their job objectives, allowing them to measure their accomplishments and illustrate the value that they place on the HIV/AIDS-related work as being on an equal level with their other bank-related work. In Bangkok, when a champion needs to be away from the office for a day or two to conduct a training session in the community, the head of corporate affairs notifies his or her boss, illustrating the high level of support for those activities.

In 2004, Standard Chartered Bank Chairman Mervyn Davies launched the HIV Ambassador Network within the bank, consisting of 20 senior executives who use their positions as prominent people in the international business community to tell the story of Standard Chartered Bank's involvement and to influence global policy on HIV/AIDS. The HIV ambassadors encourage other top executives around the world to engage in the fight against HIV/AIDS and make sure that the business case for such engagement is well understood.

Decision-Making Process

The decision to make a strong commitment to fighting the spread of HIV/AIDS ultimately comes from the bank's commitment to ensuring a healthy, stable workforce. In the 1990s, many companies started to see rapidly rising infection rates in some important markets, such as China, India, and Nigeria. Employees were getting sick or having to take care of sick family members, and it was taking a harsh business toll. They were worried about losing productivity and losing trained workers, and they estimated that the cost of treating rising numbers of employees with antiretroviral treatment would be enormous. For Standard Chartered Bank, which places high importance on its employees' wellbeing, the potential impact on employee morale was also an important concern.

Despite being a British bank, Standard Chartered feels a strong connection to the overseas communities where it has been operating, in some places for generations. There was a general sense that anything affecting the communities where the bank operates also affects the bank. The bank's board decided that a strong commitment was necessary, and the staff have been supportive of that decision and eager to get involved themselves.

The bank made a commitment to fighting HIV/AIDS in every market where it has a presence because it is truly a global challenge, but it has also found that it needs to be careful to avoid negative associations and repercussions. For example, while it implements the Living with HIV training program in the Middle East, it has to make sure that the content and the approach are culturally appropriate. For that reason, the bank's headquarters provides general guidance on and a framework for HIV/AIDS-related activities but leaves it to local branches to implement the activities in accordance with local norms and cultures, a practice that is consistent with the bank's overall approach to business.

Impact

The impact of Standard Chartered Bank's HIV/AIDS-related activities has been most visible in its offices in Africa, where large numbers of employees were absent from work or leaving their jobs because they themselves were ill or they were taking care of sick family members. As other companies have found as well, creating an environment in which HIV-positive employees can receive treatment and continue to be productive and free from the stigma associated with the disease has been an important key to retaining employees for Standard Chartered Bank.

Standard Chartered Bank has also found that its HIV/AIDS programs have had a tremendous impact on morale in the workplace. Many employees feel a sense of pride that their company is clearly not only paying lip service to the cause but is actually practicing what it preaches through its in-house and external training programs. This is especially true in Thailand, where half of university-graduate applicants say that the bank's commitment to corporate social responsibility is their reason for wanting to work at Standard Chartered Bank rather than any other bank.

Interviews

Siriporn Anunpanakul, Senior Manager, CEO Support & Administration, Standard Chartered Bank, Bangkok

Saofang Ekaluckrujee, Vice President for Corporate Affairs, Standard Chartered Bank, Bangkok

Mee Har Foo, Chief Executive Officer, Standard Chartered Bank, Bangkok

Richard Meddings, Group Finance Director, Standard Chartered Bank, London

Busba Virochpoka, Senior Executive Vice President, Corporate Affairs, Standard Chartered Bank, Bangkok

Taisei Construction Corporation
Bridge to Health

Taisei Corporation is a leading Japanese construction company founded in 1917. It has undertaken numerous domestic public works projects, including the construction of subways and airports, as well as the world's longest tunnel, which connects Japan's main island to its northernmost island, Hokkaido. The company is also actively engaged in numerous overseas projects, mainly in neighboring Asian countries.

Since February 2006, Taisei has incorporated an HIV/AIDS prevention program for construction workers into one such project, the Can Tho Bridge construction project in Vietnam. The Japan Bank for International Cooperation (JBIC),[1] which is providing the financing in the form of yen loans as a part of Japan's official development assistance (ODA) to Vietnam, has begun to recommend the inclusion of HIV/AIDS programs in construction contracts for such ODA-financed projects. The initiative is being implemented in partnership with international nongovernmental organizations (NGOs) and local public health authorities, and has expanded beyond the construction workers to include other high-risk groups such as commercial sex workers in Can Tho City and surrounding areas.

Types of activities related to HIV/AIDS

- HIV/AIDS prevention education for workers involved in the construction of the Can Tho Bridge in Vietnam
- HIV/AIDS prevention education for commercial sex workers in Can Tho City and its surrounding areas
- Distribution of condoms to construction workers and commercial sex workers

1. Management of JBIC's ODA projects was transferred to the Japan International Cooperation Agency (JICA) in October 2008, after the research for this case study was completed. All references made to JBIC in this report concern the operations of the agency before these projects were absorbed by JICA.

- Training of commercial sex workers as peer educators
- Training for local health providers
- Distribution of a guidebook on local health and medical services

HIV infection in Vietnam originally spread among injecting drug users in southern cities and provinces, many of whom had been using heroin since the war with the United States. It subsequently spread to other regions and from injecting drug users to commercial sex workers, who then passed it on to their other clients, eventually leading to widespread infection among women and children at large. By the end of 1998, HIV infections had been reported in 64 cities and provinces, and according to statistics from the Vietnamese Ministry of Health, by 2007 the number of people living with HIV had reached 290,000.[2] The vast majority of cases today are among injecting drug users and commercial sex workers, with the largest number of cases occurring among those in their 20s. The main causes of transmission in Vietnam have been identified as drug injection with unsanitary needles and unprotected commercial sex. These behaviors have been found to be common among young migrant workers, making the need for preventive measures clear. In line with these trends, infection has also been on the rise in Can Tho City—where the bridge construction project is underway—most notably among young people.

The Can Tho Bridge Construction Project

The Can Tho Bridge construction project began in 2004 to improve Vietnam's National Highway 1, which is the sole national arterial roadway linking the north and south. Can Tho City, with a population of 1.81 million and located 167 kilometers southwest of Ho Chi Minh City, is the most important hub within the Mekong River Delta region for distribution of rice and other agricultural products. However, without a bridge, travelers on Highway 1 have had to take a ferry from the neighboring province to Can Tho City, creating devastating bottlenecks that affect the region's economic growth. Once the bridge is completed, it will be the longest cable-stayed bridge in Southeast Asia and will reduce the time required to cross the river from 50 minutes to just 5 minutes.

2. WHO, UNAIDS, and UNICEF, "Epidemiological Fact Sheet on HIV and AIDS: Core Data on Epidemiology and Response: Viet Nam," December 2008, apps.who.int/globalatlas/predefinedReports/EFS2008/full/EFS2008_VN.pdf.

HIV/AIDS Prevention Programs in Large-Scale Infrastructure Projects

Development agencies have begun to express concern about the impact of construction projects supported by Japan on the spread of HIV/AIDS in the countries they are meant to assist. Large-scale infrastructure projects often rely not only on local workers but also on migrant workers from within and outside the host country. These migrant workers have been identified, along with injecting drug users and commercial sex workers, as being among the most vulnerable to HIV infection. One factor is the diversity in their knowledge about HIV/AIDS, education levels, and language abilities, placing them at a disadvantage compared with local residents, who are more likely to benefit from social welfare policies, including measures to combat HIV infection. Furthermore, although their construction jobs are generally temporary, the steady cash income and separation from their families often lead to risky behaviors, such as visiting commercial sex workers and using drugs. Tragically, many of them return home without realizing that they are infected, and therefore unknowingly spread the virus in their home communities.

JBIC gradually started to recognize that while yen loan programs can have a positive impact on the economic development of countries in the region, they can also have this type of negative side effect. The agency, therefore, decided to implement pilot measures to integrate HIV prevention programs for construction workers in large-scale projects for which it provides financing.[3] Since 2002, JBIC has explicitly included considerations for addressing communicable diseases such as HIV/AIDS into its operating policy by establishing a set of "Guidelines for Confirmation of Environmental and Social Considerations."[4]

In March 2005, JBIC began including an HIV/AIDS-related clause (stipulating the contractor's responsibility to implement HIV prevention programs for construction workers and others) in the bidding documents for large-scale, ODA-financed, public works projects in countries with HIV infection rates above a certain level. As of 2010, more than 60 yen-loan projects have incorporated HIV prevention programs. JBIC recommends that programs reflect the local context and needs and be

3. The pilot measures included HIV prevention programs for construction workers in Cambodia, Lao PDR, and Thailand, in addition to the Can Tho Bridge project in Vietnam.
4. The guidelines can be found at www.jica.go.jp/english/publications/jbic_archive/environmental_guidelines/pdf/guide.pdf.

carried out in partnership with NGOs, local health authorities, and people living with HIV/AIDS. It also recommends that the programs go beyond simply a one-way provision of information; they should encourage behavior change, involve peer educators, and incorporate social marketing strategies.

Can Tho Bridge Construction Project's HIV/AIDS Program

Corporate-NGO partnership

It is in this context that Taisei, one of the primary contractors for the Can Tho Bridge construction project (the others being Kajima and Nippon Steel, creating the "TKN Joint Operation"), developed its HIV/AIDS prevention and education program. HIV/AIDS is completely outside of Taisei's field of expertise, and it did not have any local offices in the Can Tho area. It therefore needed to create a network of people with expertise on HIV/AIDS, local medical institutions, local government authorities, and members of the local community to implement the program, and it found that NGOs were key to filling in the missing pieces. Taisei formed a partnership with the Japan branch of CARE International and its counterpart in Vietnam to launch its HIV/AIDS prevention and education program in February 2006 (see table 1).

Table 1: Outline of "Bridge to Health" program

Program period	February 2006 to February 2009
Target populations	• Workers at the bridge construction project (males, average age in mid-20s, total of about 600,000 people) • Employees of Japanese and local subcontractors (total of about 90,000 people) • Residents of areas near the project site and commercial sex workers • Employees of government and local administrative bodies • Healthcare providers (employees of local AIDS centers and of the project site infirmary)
Client	TKN Joint Operation
Implementing partners	CARE International Japan, CARE International in Vietnam
Budget	US$150,000 (¥17.25 million at US$1 = ¥115)

Compiled and updated by the Friends of the Global Fund, Japan, based on materials prepared by Hiroshi Oshima.

CARE is one of world's leading NGOs in international development. Founded in the United States in 1945, it operates programs related to empowerment, health, the environment, and education in 70 countries in Africa, Asia, Latin America, the Middle East, and Eastern Europe. CARE is a global confederation of 12 national member organizations, and CARE International Japan was created in 1987 to promote education, reconstruction efforts, health, and hygiene throughout Asia. Taisei chose CARE as its partner for several reasons: First, CARE Japan had a good grasp of the HIV/AIDS issues faced by workers in Vietnam. In 2001, CARE Japan conducted a survey of HIV/AIDS prevention among workers in Vietnam,[5] and it was among the NGOs actively calling for the inclusion of HIV/AIDS prevention programs in contracts for large-scale infrastructure projects supported by Japan. CARE Vietnam, on the other hand, has worked closely with the Vietnam Chamber of Commerce and Industry on HIV/AIDS prevention and education and has strong ties with Vietnam's business sector. Furthermore, CARE USA already had experience conducting HIV/AIDS prevention and education programs in partnership with American apparel company Timberland for workers employed in its factory in Vietnam, laying the groundwork for the organization's work with foreign companies in this area. In addition to this track record, having an office in Japan made CARE an ideal implementing partner for this program, enabling smooth communication with Taisei headquarters.

Implementation

The HIV/AIDS prevention program is implemented on a three-tier system: the activities are implemented by CARE International in Vietnam; Taisei and member companies of the TKN Joint Operation provide management; and the overall direction is decided by a steering committee that includes local authorities. In addition to Taisei Finance and Administration Manager Hiroshi Oshima, who is responsible for the overall management of the program, a local employee, Hunh Ngoc Minh, is also involved.[6] Minh handles coordination with CARE International in Vietnam and other relevant parties, such as the local HIV/AIDS center. Minh's main responsibility is the procurement of materials for the construction project,

5. CARE Japan and JICA. *HIV/AIDS Prevention Measures for Workers in Vietnam: Survey on Formation of Private Sector Proposed Projects and Multi-sectoral Partnership*, 2001.
6. All titles and affiliations listed are as of the time that this research was conducted.

but he reports that work related to the HIV/AIDS program accounts for about 30 percent of his workload. CARE International in Vietnam, as the implementing partner, is responsible for planning, developing, operating, and managing program activities. It has established an office with three full-time employees in Can Tho for this purpose.

The orientation of the program and contents of its activities are determined together with representatives of the local health center, the Ministry of Transportation, and CARE International in Vietnam. The steering committee meets twice a year to discuss the building of stronger cooperative relationships, assess progress, and consider future directions. In addition, the program implementing team meets once a month to consider the details of the activities. This meeting serves as a forum for the provision of information about prevention of HIV infection and other types of sexually transmitted infections (STIs), as well as for capacity building among those involved. The team helps provide information about HIV/AIDS to local residents by broadcasting its meetings on a local television channel.

Activities[7]

The program has four major objectives: (1) increase the capacity of company health staff and associated healthcare providers at the construction site; (2) increase the availability of information on HIV/AIDS and raise awareness in high-risk areas near the construction site, including the entertainment district; (3) form a network with the local community for an effective referral system; and (4) increase condom availability and use. The US$150,000 budget for the program has been included as part of the total contract amount of US$191,862,006.[8]

Activities targeting construction workers:

HIV/AIDS lectures at monthly safety meetings

At the beginning of every month, all of the construction workers at the project site assemble for a meeting where they receive guidance about safety on the job, including HIV/AIDS prevention. CARE staff participate in the meetings, using games and quizzes to convey easy-to-follow explanations about HIV/AIDS and instructions on preventing

7. Implementation and results of the HIV/AIDS prevention program are based on information obtained between November 2006 and February 2007.
8. The TKN Joint Operation continued the HIV/AIDS prevention program even after the construction project ended, spending another US$50,000 of its own funds from September 2008 to April 2009.

infection. They also provide information about voluntary counseling and testing and preventing other STIs.

Newsletters
A newsletter with information on HIV/AIDS in Vietnamese and English is distributed every month to everyone involved in the construction. The newsletter is also distributed to workers at two other nearby bridge construction sites financed by JBIC.

Question boxes
Question boxes have been set up at several locations (generally guardhouses) on the construction site for the submission of questions about HIV/AIDS and other STIs. Questions are replied to individually or in the monthly newsletter.

Posters
About 160 posters encouraging condom use and prevention of HIV/AIDS and other STIs have been hung around on the construction site and in residential areas where workers, site managers, and subcontractors live.

Distribution of condoms
Condoms are distributed free of charge by CARE staff at the monthly safety meetings.

Activities at the community level:

Distribution of condoms, installation of vending machines
During the first year of the program, condoms were distributed free of charge at 10 karaoke bars and "café-oms," where commercial sex work is carried out. After the first year, Taisei adopted a social marketing strategy, under which condoms were no longer available free of charge, and it began exploring the feasibility of installing a vending machine.

Training of peer educators
Since commercial sex workers are at high risk of becoming infected with HIV by sexual transmission with multiple clients, training is provided on a monthly basis to approximately 30 peer educators. The training provides information about prevention of HIV/AIDS and other STIs as well as guidance on negotiation skills to persuade clients of commercial sex facilities to use condoms. A total of 92 commercial sex workers were trained in the course of one year.

Workshop on establishing a referral system
A workshop was held for local health workers on establishing a referral system for HIV/AIDS treatment.

Guidebook on health and medical services
A guidebook on health and medical services available in Can Tho City, which included a listing of information on HIV testing (location of health centers conducting the testing, fees, etc.), was distributed (1,000 copies) to construction and commercial sex workers.

Training for local health providers
Training was offered to 30 health providers in and around Can Tho City to enhance their knowledge of HIV/AIDS and increase their counseling capacity.

Impact and Expectations

The program targets a wide range of people, from those directly involved in the construction project to commercial sex workers in the neighboring community. Immediately after the program was initiated, the local HIV/AIDS center increased the number of its staff, and other organizations in the community became involved as well. Although it is still too early to assess the long-term impact of the program, the following accomplishments have been observed, according to a survey conducted by CARE Vietnam at the end of the first year.

Increased knowledge about HIV/AIDS
Knowledge about HIV/AIDS, including how it is transmitted and how it can be prevented, improved considerably among 80 percent of the people targeted by the program. On average, about 1,000 copies of newsletters are distributed every month and a total of 85 questions were submitted during the course of one year.

Expanded use of condoms
Approximately 85,000 condoms were distributed to construction workers and others living in and around the construction site during the course of a year. As a result, use of condoms during sexual intercourse increased from 26 percent of the target population before the program to 50 percent once the program was underway. The ratio of people who had never used a condom dropped from 24 percent to 7 percent after the program was initiated.

Educational activities in the local community
Condoms and information on preventing HIV and other STIs are now available in approximately 70 percent of commercial sex outlets located near the construction site. A total of 1,000 copies of the guidebook on health and medical services were distributed, and 92 commercial sex workers underwent training to become peer educators. As many as 80 participants from 30 organizations took part in a workshop to establish a referral system, and 30 health providers were trained to enhance their knowledge on HIV/AIDS and increase their counseling skills.

One feature of this program is that it makes use of the distinctive resources of a construction company and its cooperation with the community for the sake of continuous, effective intervention. Because of the dangers inherent in construction, companies in this industry have an especially high awareness of the need to maintain safety and good health at job sites. They have already laid the groundwork and developed the institutional capacity to conduct safety-promotion measures through their monthly safety meetings and other means. By incorporating HIV/AIDS prevention into this framework, it is possible for them to conduct a sustained, effective program directed at local and migrant workers. Not only does the program benefit construction workers, it also has a positive impact on Can Tho City itself. Because infrastructure projects generally last for only two to four years, it is said to be harder for construction companies to establish a presence and make a long-term contribution in countries and regions where they operate than it is for manufacturers, which often become part of the local community. Programs like this, however, conducted in partnership with NGOs that have links to the community, have the potential to be sustained and further developed even after the project is completed, and continued coordination should be considered to ensure that this will be the case.

As mentioned above, implementation of this program was stipulated by the project contract, and there was not widespread awareness and understanding of the significance of the issue within Taisei at the beginning. However, Taisei's site manager, Hiroshi Oshima, already had some knowledge of the HIV/AIDS risk. When he was heading a bridge construction project in Cambodia in 1997, he was contacted by an international NGO in the area that wanted to conduct prevention and education activities at the site, opening his eyes to the risk. Aware of the increasing rate of HIV infection in Vietnam and around the world, he understood the need for HIV/AIDS prevention activities at the Can

Tho site. He also noted the growth of commercial sex facilities in the area surrounding the site following the start of the construction and recognized both the risks that HIV/AIDS posed to the business as well as the need for countermeasures (see figure 1). Although it took some time at first for the company's headquarters in Japan to understand the connection between the construction project and HIV/AIDS, Taisei is now actively promoting awareness of HIV/AIDS prevention programs both inside and outside the company. In 2008, Taisei launched another JBIC-financed project, this one to construct a highway in the southern part of Sri Lanka, and it is conducting an HIV/AIDS prevention program as part of that contract as well.

Figure 1: Risks to business from HIV/AIDS

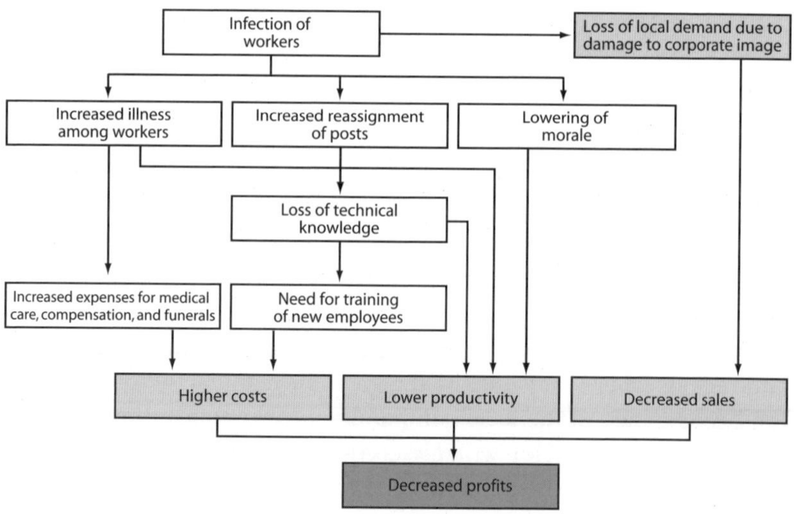

Source: CARE Japan and JICA (2001).

Oshima insists that it is not acceptable for Taisei to leave behind a negative legacy—namely, the spread of HIV/AIDS—after building the infrastructure that is intended to contribute to the economic development of the region. The company's implementation of this program is in line with its commitment to corporate social responsibility and has been the focus of attention among bilateral and multilateral development agencies working in Vietnam. It has also gathered much attention from the Japanese business sector and was selected as a location for a site visit by a mission organized by Japan's Council for Better Corporate Citizenship in September 2007, offering the opportunity for an intense exchange of ideas between the corporate social responsibility officers of various Japanese companies who took part in the mission and representatives of Taisei, JBIC, and CARE International in Vietnam.[9] The program thus promises to be an exemplary case for other companies undertaking major infrastructure construction projects and factory operations in countries and regions highly affected by HIV/AIDS.

Interviews

Hiroshi Oshima, Finance and Administration Manager, Taisei Corporation

Kouichirou Shimamoto, Chief Manager, Planning & Administration Section; CSR Promotion Section, Corporate Planning Department, Taisei Corporation

Masami Miyauchi, Project Manager, Can Tho Bridge Project, Taisei Corporation

Tatsuo Watanabe, Manager, CSR Promotion Section, Corporate Planning Department, Taisei Corporation

Hunh Ngoc Minh, Procurement Officer, TKN Joint Operation

Dinh Xuan Lam, Project Manger, Can Tho Office, CARE International Vietnam

Troung Quang Hong, Health Training & IEC Coordinator, Ho Chi Minh City Office, CARE International Vietnam

Le Thanh Liem, Can Tho Bridge Project Manager, My Thuan Project Management Unit, Ministry of Transportation and Communication

Lai Kim Anh, Director, Center of HIV/AIDS Control, Can Tho Department of Health Center

Yuho Hayakawa, Director, Social Development Division, Sector Strategy Development Department, JBIC

Emi Inaoka, Social Development Specialist (Health), Social Development Division, Sector Strategy Development Department, JBIC

Yoshie Muramatsu, Program Director, CARE International Japan

---

9. For more information on the mission, see Council for Better Corporate Citizenship (CBCC). *CBCC Mission to Vietnam: Report on the Corporate Social Responsibility in Vietnam*, 2008.

Levi Strauss and Company
Taking Chances and Taking the Lead

Levi Strauss and Company (LS&CO) is an apparel manufacturer founded by Levi Strauss, an immigrant from Bavaria, as a dry-goods store in 1853. Having moved to San Francisco during the gold rush, Strauss and a tailor from Nevada began making sturdy working clothes for miners, which would later become the famous Levi's jeans. As of the end of 2009, LS&CO employed more than 11,800 workers in its operations in more than 40 countries, and its products were being sold in 110 countries around the world.[1]

Within a year of setting up his first store in San Francisco, Strauss made a donation to a local orphanage, and he and the company he built have continued that spirit of philanthropy and social contribution ever since. Through its social contributions, the company aims to provide underserved communities where it operates with access to healthcare and education. In 1897, Strauss endowed 28 scholarships at the University of California, Berkeley, which are still in place today. The company also has a long tradition of commitment to inclusion and diversity. When it bought a factory in Virginia in 1960, for example, it integrated the facility—four years before the Civil Rights Act made segregation illegal.

This pioneering and philanthropic spirit made it only natural that the company would become one of the first to tackle the HIV/AIDS challenge that began to shake American society in the 1980s. In the early stages of the epidemic, as new cases of HIV/AIDS were being detected all over the United States, San Francisco was one of the areas hardest hit. For LS&CO, the virus was challenging its workforce and the very community in which it stood.

1. LS&CO, *Levi Strauss & Co. 2009 Annual Report*, 9, 19, 23.

Types of activities related to HIV/AIDS

- Workplace practices aimed at raising awareness of HIV prevention
- Outreach to other companies
- Awareness raising among the general public
- Grantmaking
- Harm reduction through support for a syringe-exchange program
- Encouraging employee volunteerism

In 1982, the year after the first AIDS diagnoses were made, a group of employees in LS&CO's San Francisco headquarters requested permission from the senior management committee to distribute educational materials on HIV/AIDS to their colleagues in the headquarters lobby. The committee was concerned that the lack of information and the stigma associated with the disease would prevent some employees from comfortably asking questions or taking literature. So, they decided to allow the employees to carry out their plan of distributing materials and took a significant additional step of joining the group in distributing materials in the lobby. By doing so, the company's senior management was able to demonstrate the importance that the company placed on making sure that its employees had accurate information and to illustrate to all of their staff that no one should be afraid to talk about HIV/AIDS. The following year, LS&CO became one of the first companies to develop comprehensive HIV/AIDS education and health services for its employees and their families. On top of that, since 1992 it has offered full medical benefits to unmarried partners of its employees, the first major company in the United States to do so.

The company has also helped other companies and organizations develop workplace policies on HIV/AIDS. As early as 1986, it hosted a conference on "AIDS in the Workplace" with 200 participants from 100 companies, offering a forum for companies to exchange ideas and concerns about how they handle HIV/AIDS issues in the workplace. Later, in 2001, the International Labor Organization (ILO) invited LS&CO to represent American businesses in a meeting in Geneva to develop the "ILO Code of Practice on HIV/AIDS and the World of Work," which was announced the following year. One important accomplishment that the company achieved in the meeting was to convince the ILO to insert language in its code of practice that expanded the interpretation of discrimination. In the new interpretation, not only was workplace discrimination based on perceived serostatus banned, but the code went one step further to ban assumptions of serostatus based on sexual orientation.

Having already made a strong commitment to fighting the spread of HIV and the challenge of stigma and discrimination among its employees and within the communities where it operates, LS&CO has expanded its activities to promote AIDS awareness more widely. It uses part of its marketing budget and its marketing expertise to educate young people in the United States and abroad on HIV/AIDS, offering messages of prevention and stigma reduction and encouraging young people to get involved in the fight against HIV/AIDS through their own personal behavior as well as through a variety of volunteer activities.

Philanthropic and social initiatives are not new to LS&CO, which has articulated four values—empathy, originality, integrity, and courage—as pillars of its company philosophy. In 1952, the company established the Levi Strauss Foundation to address a wide range of social issues. HIV/AIDS is one of the foundation's priority areas, and since 1985 the foundation has given away more than US$38 million to support AIDS-related activities. Within this field, it focuses on three areas: (1) reducing stigma and discrimination associated with HIV infection; (2) supporting communities that have been hit hard by HIV as well as underserved communities; and (3) providing injecting drug users with access to clean syringes.

Volunteerism is another important pillar of the company's approach to dealing with the challenges of HIV/AIDS in the communities where it operates. Since the early days of its creation, LS&CO has encouraged its employees to contribute to their own communities through volunteerism and social contributions. Since the 1970s, employees have been getting involved through the company's Community Involvement Teams (CITs), company-sponsored, employee-led groups that volunteer with organizations in their communities. The company provides the CITs with venues for planning meetings for their volunteer activities. In the United States, all of its full-time employees are given up to five hours per month of paid time off to perform volunteer work. The company also encourages employee and retiree donations by fully matching their contributions to qualified organizations and making grants to organizations in which employees and retirees volunteer their time. The company's approach to supporting communities even inspired Jerry O'Shea, a former employee who decided with his wife in 1981 to create the Red Tab Foundation, which helps LS&CO employees and retirees provide for their basic needs and those of their families when they have been faced with unexpected emergencies.

Examples of LS&CO employee volunteer activities in the HIV/AIDS field include employees in the San Francisco headquarters who deliver meals to AIDS patients; employees in the Philippines who conduct HIV/AIDS storytelling workshops in schools, offices, and organizations; and employees in Hong Kong who work with the Boys and Girls Clubs Association to educate the younger generation about HIV/AIDS, to name only a few.[2]

Reaching Out to Young People in South Africa

LS&CO operations around the world operate their own awareness-raising campaigns with relative autonomy, something that is respected by the company's top management in San Francisco.

Through its clothing lines, LS&CO aims to reach a young, hip, urban market. In South Africa, a country with one of the world's highest HIV infection rates, LS&CO uses that influence to educate young people about the risks of HIV/AIDS and how they can protect themselves from infection. For example, Levi Strauss South Africa decided to use part of its marketing budget to combine its goal of selling jeans with its goal of raising awareness about HIV/AIDS, and it chose to do so through music. In 2005, it partnered with the Treatment Action Campaign South Africa to launch the Red for Life campaign. The campaign began with a concert in February 2005 that brought in some of South Africa's biggest names in music. Before it began organizing the concerts, there was a lot of skepticism over whether prominent musicians would be willing to publicly associate themselves with a concert on such a controversial topic as AIDS, but they found that the performers were eager to get involved. More than 3,000 young people attended the concert, and more than 60,000 free condoms were distributed in schools, stores, and other venues as a part of the campaign.[3] The second concert in the series was held in October 2006.

In 2005, the Red for Life campaign also created a documentary to be broadcast on World AIDS Day. In the documentary, *Unzipped*, famous actors and musicians talked very bluntly about their sexual experiences

---

2. Community Involvement Teams, LS&CO website, www.levistrauss.com/Citizenship/CommunityInvolvement/CommunityInvolvementTeams.aspx.
3. Global Business Coalition on HIV/AIDS (GBC), *Outstanding Business Action of HIV/AIDS: Case Studies—2005*. (New York: GBC, 2005), 19.

and about the importance of using condoms to protect against HIV infection. While they might have been uncomfortable talking about such intimate details, the celebrities who participated in the documentary said that it was important not to sugarcoat messages about HIV/AIDS and safe sex even if it might make some of the parents uncomfortable. Instead, they wanted to be much more direct to make sure that young people got the message about the critical importance of using condoms and understanding safe sex.[4]

Cultivating the HIV/AIDS Community in Japan

Levi Strauss Japan (LSJ) is a pioneer in the field of corporate support for AIDS, becoming the first corporation in Japan to engage in the fight against the spread of HIV/AIDS as early as the 1990s, when Japanese corporate interest in the issue was still very low.

In Japan, as in other countries, the company's efforts related to HIV/AIDS originally centered around the efforts of CIT members, who have created original condom cases out of scrap material from Levi's jeans, produced and distributed T-shirts with educational messages on HIV prevention, and provided education on prevention to young people, the core of the company's market. Most outstanding is the financial support that has been extended to Japanese nongovernmental organizations (NGOs) involved in domestic HIV/AIDS issues, particularly in a country like Japan where corporate support for NGOs is relatively low compared with many other countries. Over the years, the Levi Strauss Foundation has provided long-term financial support to domestic Japanese NGOs that support people living with HIV/AIDS and that educate people on prevention. With the financial resources coming from the Levi Strauss Foundation, the company has been able to experiment with several approaches to grantmaking in Japan, including encouraging employee participation and working through intermediaries.

When the Levi Strauss Foundation began making grants in Japan, a team of volunteers was responsible for choosing the grantees. Employees themselves went out to find NGOs that were starting to get involved in AIDS work and made grants to them. Because the employees themselves

4. "Stars Tell Sex Secrets on TV; New Documentary Gets Celebs to Share Their Hottest Moments with Viewers," *Sunday Times of South Africa*, November 20, 2005, www.aegis.com/news/suntimes/2005/ST051106.html.

were taking a very proactive approach, it also gave them an opportunity to meet face-to-face with the AIDS community and form relationships. Given that LSJ was the first corporation to fund AIDS-related work in Japan, many NGO staff still have clear memories of getting to know LSJ employees and witnessing their enthusiasm.

As Japan's civil society sector was growing and institutionalizing, the foundation found that it needed to develop more expertise and take a more wide-reaching approach to its grantmaking in Japan. Accordingly, in 1997 it created a donor advised fund with the Japan Center for International Exchange (JCIE), known as the Levi Strauss Foundation Advised Fund of JCIE. Approximately ¥20 million was awarded annually to Japanese NGOs that were promoting social justice. During the seven years that the fund was in operation, it gave roughly ¥35 million (US$292,000)—or about a quarter of its total funding—in grants to NGOs that educate people about HIV prevention and provide support to people living with HIV/AIDS.[5] This partnership brought in a Japanese intermediary organization—one with a firm grasp of the context and actual needs of the target communities—to take over the management of the grantmaking program, with the aim of engaging the company in more effective grantmaking.

In communities around the world where LS&CO has a business interest, the Levi Strauss Foundation supports NGOs, using common guidelines and targeting the same general fields. However, because the context and needs are different in each country, the foundation's priority activities vary accordingly so that its grants can be more effective locally. JCIE was careful to respect the will and desired outcomes of the corporation and the foundation—the funders—while striving for grantmaking activities that were appropriate to the Japanese context. Compared with NGOs in Europe and North America, the organizational and financial base for NGOs in Japan is relatively weak, raising different concerns in the grantmaking process.

In 2004, having cultivated a network of Japanese NGOs dealing with AIDS and having developed its own knowledge about Japan's civil society sector, the foundation's Asia Pacific regional office began making grants to organizations in Japan directly. Grants were still made in the three target fields of HIV/AIDS prevention, economic empowerment, and social justice for workers in the apparel industry, but greater focus

5. In addition to HIV/AIDS, the Levi Strauss Foundation Advised Fund of JCIE also made grants for youth education and social justice. The full amount of funding in all three fields totaled ¥130 million (approximately US$1.08 million).

was given to NGOs involved in HIV/AIDS issues in the case of Japan. Working with a consultant who is knowledgeable about Japan's HIV/AIDS NGOs, the foundation is carrying out small but strategic grantmaking by invitation only. By providing more than US$100,000 in grants annually, the foundation continues to contribute to the development of Japan's HIV/AIDS community. In 2007, for example, grants totaling US$135,000 were awarded in Japan to organizations focused on preventing HIV/AIDS among youth through peer education and on reducing HIV/AIDS-related stigma and discrimination.

Taking Chances: Harm Reduction

Injecting drug use has been identified as the leading cause of HIV transmission in many parts of the United States. Eager to address the real challenges to fighting the spread of HIV infection in the United States, the Levi Strauss Foundation created the Syringe Access Fund in 2004, in partnership with the Tides Foundation (also located in San Francisco) and the National AIDS Fund. The Syringe Access Fund provides grants of up to US$100,000 each for syringe-exchange programs and education efforts. The fund has grown rapidly since 2004 with the introduction of new donors including the Elton John AIDS Foundation. The foundation also extended its grantmaking for harm reduction programs in other countries. In 2005, it made grants to organizations in Indonesia and Thailand that are working with injecting drug users.

The Syringe Access Fund responds to a need for what is commonly referred to as harm reduction—still a controversial issue in the United States and abroad. The concept of harm reduction is that we should mitigate the risks that injecting drug users pose to themselves and to their sexual partners in spreading HIV and other infections by providing sterile needles and syringes rather than trying to completely eliminate the use of drugs or stopping people from injecting. Although most people still believe that reducing or even eliminating illegal drug use from our society should remain a high priority, this is unlikely to happen in the near future. Therefore, harm reduction programs offer a more practical solution by addressing the reality that HIV infection continues to spread rapidly while efforts are being made to stop illegal drug use. Although critics claim that such programs only encourage people to use drugs, there appears to be no evidence to support this claim, and on the contrary, there is strong evidence that the spread of HIV infection among injecting drug users has decreased in cities around the world that have implemented syringe-exchange programs, and in some cases risky injecting behavior has been reduced by as much as 73 percent.[6] Still, there is a great deal of stigma associated with drug use in general, so funders are hesitant to risk getting involved in such a controversial area as harm reduction. The Levi Strauss Foundation is the first corporate funder to openly fund such a program.

Because of the controversy surrounding harm reduction, the Levi Strauss Foundation board wanted to tread carefully and make sure that they were fully prepared for any criticism. They invited a representative from the corporate communications department to help them articulate in advance responses to complaints they anticipated hearing. They based their response on five principles:

- *Evidence*: There is clear evidence from respected organizations such as the Centers for Disease Control and Prevention (CDC) that harm reduction strategies save lives and drastically reduce HIV and other blood-borne infections.
- *Legality*: Although drug use is illegal in the United States, legal organizations support the implementation of harm reduction strategies.
- *Cost*: According to the CDC, a clean syringe costs 7 cents, but treatment for a person who becomes infected with HIV can cost between US$4,000 and US$12,000 per year.
- *Police acceptance*: Although some people have argued that police officers do not like syringe-exchange programs and other harm reduction strategies, Levi Strauss Foundation staff have found that the police do, in fact, prefer to have clean needles on the streets rather than dirty ones.
- *Affect on drug use*: Levi Strauss Foundation staff found that they could illustrate that providing clean syringes does not increase drug use by pointing out to their critics in the non-using community that if someone were to hand them a syringe, that act would not prompt them to start using drugs.

In the end, neither the Levi Strauss Foundation nor the company itself has received any criticism for their involvement in the Syringe Access Fund since it was launched. However, the exercise of determining ahead of time what their reaction would be if they did receive

6. Syringe Access Fund, Levi Strauss Foundation website, www.levistrauss.com/Citizenship/LeviStraussFoundation/SyringeAccessFund.aspx.

criticism proved to be useful in clarifying the company's commitment to the cause internally.

LS&CO is widely known as one of the first companies to make bold, public commitments to fighting the spread of HIV/AIDS and tackling issues of stigma and discrimination head on. As the HIV/AIDS field continues to evolve and grow, the company will no doubt continue to play a leadership role in this field.

Interviews

Satoshi Adachi, Product Integrity, Raw Materials Leader, Business Planning and Control, Supply Chain Department, LSJ

Keiji Amemiya, Communication Manager, Marketing Service Department, LSJ

Stuart Burden, Director, Community Affairs—the Americas, LS&CO and Levi Strauss Foundation

M·A·C Cosmetics
Dedication to a Powerful Brand Image

M·A·C (Make-Up Art Cosmetics) was established in Toronto, Canada, in 1985 by make-up artists Frank Toskan and Frank Angelo. M·A·C Cosmetics is widely known in the make-up, entertainment, and fashion industries as one of the most popular brands of professional make up, but it also produces and markets its products to the general public for everyday use. M·A·C Cosmetics has its headquarters in New York, and its products are sold in 54 countries around the world. The brand is now a part of the Estée Lauder Companies and is its fastest-growing makeup-artist brand. Marketed solely through word-of-mouth among make-up artists and other consumers, the rapidly growing US$1 billion company relies heavily on its reputation and customer loyalty. As of 2007, M·A·C Cosmetics employed more than 9,000 people worldwide.

The M·A·C AIDS Fund was established in 1994 as a response to the devastating toll that HIV/AIDS was taking on the fashion and entertainment industries. Later that year, Viva Glam lipstick was created to support the fund. More than US$135 million had been raised as of 2009 for the M·A·C AIDS Fund through the sales of Viva Glam lipstick and lip gloss, making it America's top non-pharmaceutical corporate donor to the fight against HIV/AIDS.[1] There are six staff working for the M·A·C AIDS Fund in the company's New York headquarters.

Types of activities related to HIV/AIDS

- Grantmaking based on sales of Viva Glam lipsticks and lip glosses
- HIV awareness raising through Viva Glam spokespeople
- Kids Helping Kids gift cards, benefiting pediatric AIDS programs
- M·A·C Good Spirits make-up program for people living with HIV/AIDS
- Online information and contact information on HIV testing

1. Funders Concerned About AIDS, *US Philanthropic Support to Address HIV/AIDS in 2007* (New York: Funders Concerned About AIDS, 2008).

In 1994, recognizing the devastating toll that the spread of HIV/AIDS was having in the creative communities that use their products, the founders of M·A·C Cosmetics decided that they wanted their company to take a leading, outspoken role in the fight against HIV/AIDS. In doing so, they chose to create a new model of providing corporate support and created a special line of lipsticks for this purpose that would be sold alongside other M·A·C products. The lipsticks were called Viva Glam, and in 2006 the sixth color—Viva Glam VI—was launched. With the launch of Viva Glam V and Viva Glam VI, a lip gloss was also launched, reflecting growing consumer demand. The unique aspect of the program is that 100 percent of the retail price of every Viva Glam lipstick and lip gloss that is sold goes directly to the M·A·C AIDS Fund, and 100 percent of that money is distributed to grantees. In other words, the company itself covers all costs incurred in developing, producing, and marketing the Viva Glam products as well as all of the administrative costs incurred in the grantmaking process.

M·A·C AIDS Fund grants are made to organizations on the front lines of fighting HIV/AIDS in the United States and abroad. In the early days of the fund, support went primarily to organizations that were offering social and healthcare services to people living with HIV/AIDS. Since then, the scope of grants has expanded to include advocacy efforts to attract greater attention and resources to the disease, education to raise awareness and teach effective prevention, and capacity building to support sustained long-term responses in hard-hit areas. More recently, the fund made an inaugural grant to the Millennium Villages Project based at the Earth Institute at Columbia University, which is integrating HIV/AIDS-related work with broader poverty-alleviation and capacity-building efforts in several villages in Africa. While the fund wants to maintain its grassroots nature, as its financial size is growing rapidly it is finding that it can also invest large sums of money in larger efforts for more impact.

Funds raised by sales of Viva Glam products outside of the United States are generally allocated to organizations in the country of sale. For example, the revenue from sales of Viva Glam in Japan were used for two grants in 2006, one to the Friends of the Global Fund, Japan, to mobilize Japanese support for the Global Fund and promote cooperation with other East Asian countries in the battle against communicable diseases, and one to MTV International's Staying Alive Foundation for MTV Japan's *Think Loud* program, which aims to raise Japanese young people's awareness on a variety of social issues, including HIV/AIDS.

Staff of the M·A·C AIDS Fund and corporate staff of M·A·C Cosmetics say that the company tries to stay on the cutting edge in everything it does, from selling make-up to fighting AIDS. Within the fund, this means finding a balance between supporting organizations that are providing vital, long-term, consistent support to people infected and affected by HIV and making grants to organizations that are trying out new ways of dealing with the disease.

The M·A·C AIDS Fund decided to enlist the support of Viva Glam spokespeople—icons from the music, fashion, and entertainment industries—to market Viva Glam products around the world. In addition to helping the company market this important product, the spokespeople educate M·A·C consumers and a broader general public about HIV/AIDS—particularly about how people can protect themselves from infection and help stop the spread. Sixteen spokespeople have represented Viva Glam products as of 2007, bringing attention to the cause. The spokespeople are chosen to represent the wide diversity of M·A·C employees and consumers, giving them role models in the fight against HIV/AIDS with whom they can easily identify. The first spokesperson, in 1994, was a famous actor and drag queen by the name of RuPaul. Since then, Viva Glam spokespeople have included male and female singers, actresses, supermodels, sex symbols, and an internationally renowned burlesque dancer.

More than half of new HIV infections every year occur in youth between the ages of 15 and 24, and there are an estimated 25 million children around the world who have been orphaned by AIDS.[2] While the M·A·C market is primarily made up of adults, the company has found that it cannot ignore the incredible toll that HIV/AIDS takes on children as well. As a result, M·A·C created the Kids Helping Kids campaign, through which every year they sell gift cards and tags featuring art created by children from around the world who are infected or affected by HIV. As with Viva Glam products, 100 percent of the selling price of the cards goes to HIV/AIDS-related organizations, in this case pediatric HIV/AIDS organizations around the world.

M·A·C has also created a program to directly use its products and skills to make the lives of people living with HIV/AIDS a little better. Launched in 2002, the M·A·C Good Spirits program offers free makeovers by its professional make-up artists to men and women with HIV/AIDS. The makeovers focus on minimizing the visual effects of the disease and

2. UNAIDS, "Children and Orphans," www.unaids.org/en/PolicyAndPractice/KeyPopulations/ChildAndOrphans/.

medication on the face and neck, giving participants more confidence to interact with family and friends and live more active, more positive, healthier lives. The program is modeled after similar programs helping cancer patients to improve their self-image, based on evidence that raising self-esteem and developing a more positive outlook helps people with terminal illnesses to live longer, healthier lives.

Finally, the M·A·C AIDS Fund website offers basic information about various testing options and provides contact information in six countries for those interested in learning more about testing, which is among the most important weapons in the fight against HIV/AIDS.

The Power of a Brand Image

M·A·C uses a unique corporate giving model of creating and marketing one product specifically for fundraising purposes and providing 100 percent of the retail price to the fund. A top M·A·C Cosmetics executive has described the model as powerful because of its purity and clarity. It is easy for the make-up artists who are selling M·A·C products as well as the customers who are buying the products to understand exactly what they—as employees or as consumers—are contributing: every single penny that they bring in or pay for the product. The model also makes a bold statement about M·A·C's unwavering commitment to fighting AIDS by showing the world that they are willing to take a chance on a product line sold at a direct financial loss for the benefit of a social cause.

In more traditional product-related fundraising models, a portion of the profits from sales are donated to a cause, meaning that the costs of developing and marketing the product are recouped and the portion of the profit that is not donated is retained by the company. One might think that a model that encourages people to buy a product that will not only not bring profit to the company but will also cost the company money to develop and sell would ultimately be bad for business, but M·A·C Cosmetics has found the complete opposite to be true. Revenue from other M·A·C products has grown rapidly over the years at the same time that Viva Glam has continued to be one of the company's best-selling products.

One factor in the success of the M·A·C model is the selection of the product. Viva Glam lipsticks and lip glosses are good, solid products with fairly subdued colors that tend to be appropriate for a wide range of people and tastes. If the company tried to compromise the quality of the product, knowing that the line was not directly bringing any income to the company, they might not have the same level of success. People buy Viva Glam because they know they are contributing to a good cause, but they also buy it because it is a good product, living up to the standards they expect from a top make-up company. Also, M·A·C made a strategic decision to choose a lipstick rather than other make-up products such as foundation or blush because most people who use lipstick generally own a variety of colors rather than sticking to one or two products that they use every day. If, for example, they had chosen to create a foundation as the fundraising product, they might not have had the same level of success because they would be dependent on sales of the foundation only to consumers who happened to find that product most suitable to their own skin and taste. Many more of their consumers are willing to try a new lipstick, giving more people the opportunity to take part in the M·A·C AIDS Fund community.

Prior to the establishment of the M·A·C AIDS Fund, M·A·C Cosmetics had never used advertising to sell its products. Instead, it relied solely on word-of-mouth endorsements from the artists and others who use their products. When it launched the Viva Glam line, however, it needed to reach a larger audience in order to disseminate not only information about the new product but also its bold prevention messages. By doing so, the M·A·C AIDS Fund in a sense became the public face of M·A·C Cosmetics.

Locally Appropriate Approaches

M·A·C Cosmetics sells its products in 54 countries around the world, and Viva Glam is sold along with other M·A·C products in every one of those markets. In order to reinforce the grassroots nature of its involvement in the fight against HIV/AIDS, income from Viva Glam sales is distributed to organizations in the countries where the products are sold. Of course, every country has a different experience with HIV/AIDS, from different infection rates and general paths of transmission to different levels of awareness and comfort with prevention messages dealing with issues of safe sex and drug use. As a result, they have had to tailor their advocacy and grantmaking approaches in each country to the local norms and culture without compromising their standards of awareness raising and inclusion. In some places, that means not being quite as vocal in their advocacy messages. In others, it means finding grantees that are more mainstream than the "edgier" organizations they support in North America. M·A·C AIDS Fund staff have found that in some markets it is easier to support AIDS orphans or reduction of mother-to-child transmission—both areas in urgent need of support around the world—because mothers and children are seen as less controversial than other hard-hit communities. Through its international grantmaking, the M·A·C AIDS Fund has found that every country can make a significant contribution while focusing its prevention messages and support in a locally appropriate manner.

Staff Participation

M·A·C Cosmetics prides itself on integrating all of its staff—from the corporate offices, to the make-up artists, to the retail staff—in the efforts of the M·A·C AIDS Fund. It is ultimately the make-up artists and retail staff who are the ones encouraging their customers to buy Viva Glam products, thereby raising funds for the M·A·C AIDS Fund and raising awareness about the importance of paying attention to HIV/AIDS and about the role that M·A·C Cosmetics is playing. Information on Viva Glam products and the M·A·C AIDS Fund is integrated into all training sessions for staff so that they understand the purpose of the fund and the message that the company is trying to get across. Integrating M·A·C's HIV/AIDS-related activities into staff training sessions also helps to reinforce its policy of integrating HIV/AIDS-related programming into everything it does as a company. All M·A·C Cosmetics staff also play an important role in choosing the recipients of the funds that they, as M·A·C employees, help raise for the M·A·C AIDS Fund.

M·A·C Cosmetics has a relatively high percentage of gay and lesbian employees, representing a community that was initially hit hardest by the spread of HIV infection. The company has a reputation for being edgy and is known for the diversity of its employees. Retail staff of most cosmetics companies tend to fit certain narrow physical profiles that are meant to reflect the brands they are selling. M·A·C Cosmetics, on the other hand, explicitly employs make-up artists and retailers of all sizes, shapes, races, ethnicities, genders, orientations, and styles. This diverse public face is reflected in its selection of its spokespeople as well, from the African American drag queen RuPaul to the blond, buxom sex symbol Pamela Anderson. What they all have in common is a strong drive to fight the spread of HIV/AIDS in their own unique way.

Employee retention rates at M·A·C Cosmetics are high. An internal survey of M·A·C make-up artists asked them to provide the top three reasons why they decided to work at M·A·C Cosmetics and why they stayed with the company. The number one reason given was that employees can express their creativity in their jobs at M·A·C Cosmetics. The second reason was that they were encouraged to be themselves, something that is rare in the beauty industry. The third most common reason they gave was the commitment that M·A·C is making to fighting HIV/AIDS through the M·A·C AIDS Fund.

Impact

As with many of the other companies covered in this project, when asked about any negative impacts of their HIV/AIDS-related work on the company, M·A·C Cosmetics and M·A·C AIDS Fund executives could not think of any. For them, it has been an entirely positive experience. The Viva Glam product line and the M·A·C AIDS Fund have been integrated fully into everything M·A·C Cosmetics does and everything it stands for, and they are the key to the company's reputation. For a company that relies on word-of-mouth endorsements, the fact that the entire company has grown rapidly since the M·A·C AIDS Fund was created in 1994 illustrates that consumers are drawn to M·A·C Cosmetics and remain loyal to the brand not only because of the quality and value of the products but also because of the value of the social contribution that the company is making. In addition, the central role that the M·A·C AIDS Fund plays in attracting and retaining strong employees is invaluable to the company, as employees who are excited about the product they are selling excite their customers and, ultimately, tend to sell more products to more people.

Interviews

Peter Lichtenthal, Global General Manager, M·A·C Cosmetics
Nancy Mahon, Executive Director, M·A·C AIDS Fund

MTV
Unleashing the Power of Mass Media to Fight AIDS

Music Television (MTV) was first launched in the United States on August 1, 1981, and quickly became one of the most popular television programs for young people. Today, reaching as many as 496 million households worldwide, MTV is the most widely distributed television brand in the world. On average, MTV's HIV/AIDS-related programming reaches 64 percent of households that have televisions around the world, or approximately 1.4 billion people worldwide. Because it distributes its HIV/AIDS-related content free of charge and logo-free to other broadcasters when appropriate, this content reaches roughly 90 percent of households with televisions in the most heavily impacted areas. The HIV/AIDS-related content on its website, which has been translated into more than 10 languages—including Japanese—receives an average of about 500,000 hits per month. MTV's audience is primarily young people in the 13- to 25-year-old range.

This ability to reach such a wide audience of young people and the timeliness of the company's launch in the United States—less than two months after the first AIDS diagnosis (at the time, it was called "pneumocysitis carinii pneumonia")—meant that it was quite natural for MTV to make a strong, early commitment to fighting the spread of the disease. MTV Networks International brings music television to households in 164 countries around the world, and the company, based in London, has made fighting the spread of HIV/AIDS a top social commitment. It creates and airs its own HIV/AIDS-related programming and helps MTV networks at the country level create their own locally appropriate programming. MTV International's Staying Alive campaign on AIDS was launched in 1998.

As of 2007, MTV estimated that it was offering roughly US$50 million per year worth of free airtime—in addition to the MTV airtime commitment explained below—for HIV/AIDS-related programming. This number does not include the cost of the staff time that goes into the programming, so the real financial cost of its involvement would be even higher.

Types of activities related to HIV/AIDS

- Workplace policy
- Training on prevention for all new employees
- Public service announcements (PSAs) on safe sex
- HIV-positive characters in its programs
- Documentaries featuring people living with HIV/AIDS
- Viewer-created PSAs, short videos, and video games
- Film contest in association with the 16th International AIDS Conference
- Online interactive guide on sexual health

MTV has a workplace policy that guarantees confidentiality of serostatus, addresses stigma and discrimination based on serostatus, and supports basic education on HIV/AIDS for its employees. It also offers training for all new employees on HIV prevention.

Leveraging its ability to capture the attention of young people around the world, AIDS-related programming on MTV began with PSAs, teaching its viewers about the danger of HIV transmission and how to prevent it. It has also woven HIV/AIDS-related storylines into its programs, most notably its hit reality series, *The Real World*. In 1998, MTV Networks International, in partnership with the Joint United Nations Programme on HIV/AIDS (UNAIDS) and the World Bank, launched a documentary series about young people around the world who are infected and affected by HIV, hosted by prominent musicians. The documentary series has been reinforced by the staging of Staying Alive Concerts to garner even wider attention.

In more recent years, MTV has begun involving its audience more and more in its AIDS-related programming. In 2002, it organized and aired a Global Forum during the 14th International AIDS Conference, which was held in Barcelona, Spain. MTV and its partners selected 75 young people who were attending the conference to participate in the forum, where they were allowed to ask pointed questions of the panelists, who included US President Bill Clinton, UNAIDS Executive Director Peter Piot, actor Rupert Everett, and others. Toward the end of the forum, participants asked questions only of President Clinton, which eventually turned into an impromptu, unscripted discussion after the formal part of the forum had ended.

In 2005, MTV International's Staying Alive campaign asked its viewers to submit ideas for PSAs to be aired globally on World AIDS Day. A similar contest calling for short screenplays was held in 2006 as a part of the KNOW HIV/AIDS campaign conducted by Viacom, MTV Network's parent company. The winner of the contest was invited to develop his short film into a feature-length film, which was broadcast on MTV and other Viacom networks. The film tells the story of a young promiscuous man who does not believe that HIV can affect him until he is encouraged to take an HIV test and finds out that he is positive. In 2006, MTV launched a contest to encourage young people to film themselves talking about HIV/AIDS. The creators of the best "vlogs," as they are called, were rewarded with free video cameras, and their creations were aired globally on television and online. Also in 2006, MTV Japan, with a grant from the M·A·C AIDS Fund, launched a similar competition among youth in Japan to submit proposals for PSAs on such issues as HIV testing, stigma and discrimination, and the psycho-social issues facing Japanese youth as a result of their vulnerability to HIV infection. While in Japan to present the M·A·C AIDS Fund awards to MTV Japan and the Friends of the Global Fund, Japan, spokesmodel Pamela Anderson appeared on stage during the MTV Video Music Awards Japan to talk about the importance of HIV testing.

In January 2007, mtvU, a network broadcast to colleges and universities across the United States, launched a new contest in partnership with the Henry J. Kaiser Family Foundation, this one using the medium of video games, following the success of a video game contest focused on Darfur that was launched by mtvU and other partners. Students were invited to submit concepts for web-based video games that teach young people about the spread of HIV/AIDS and what they can do to stop it. The winning concept received a grant and other support to be turned into an online game, *Pos or Not*, which challenges the stigma connected with HIV infection while teaching prevention methods.

During the 16th International AIDS Conference in 2006, held in Toronto, Canada, MTV chose 48 young delegates to the conference who were divided into eight teams—each accompanied by one professional Canadian filmmaker—that were tasked with creating films on AIDS-themed subjects. The teams were given 48 hours to create their films, which were screened at an awards ceremony held during the conference.

The films, and a documentary about their creation, are featured on MTV International's website and were aired on MTV stations around the world.

To ensure that HIV/AIDS messages make it consistently to audiences around the world, every MTV network is required to air a minimum of one minute of HIV/AIDS-related programming every day during prime time. MTV networks in Africa and other hard-hit areas have chosen to commit even more, airing at least six minutes per day during prime time. Still, when MTV International created the Staying Alive program, it realized that it would need to reach a wider audience in Africa than it previously had. It decided, therefore, to offer the programming rights free to any broadcaster interested in airing the documentary. It also offered the option of airing the program with or without the MTV logo. This decision has allowed the network to reach people in the most-at-risk, hardest-to-reach corners of the globe.

In 1997, MTV launched "think: Sexual Health" on its website in order to offer more opportunities for its fans to learn about safe sex practices. The site includes an interactive guide to sexual health, a database of testing facilities, news on sexual health issues, a 24-hour message board for viewer discussions, and information on volunteer and peer educator opportunities. The information on the website has also been produced in booklet form, under the title *It's Your (Sex) Life*, produced in partnership with the Henry J. Kaiser Family Foundation. Young people can request copies of the free booklet through the website or by calling a toll-free number. Advocacy organizations such as Advocates for Youth, Rock the Vote, and LIFEbeat also distribute the booklet at their events. As of the end of 2006, roughly 500,000 copies had been distributed.

The Power of Mass Media in Prevention

According to a 2006 nationwide poll by the Henry J. Kaiser Family Foundation, 61 percent of Americans look first and foremost to the media (television, newspapers, radio, and the Internet) for information about HIV/AIDS.[1] MTV has long been one of the top sources of entertainment for youth (ages 13–25) in countries around the world. For many, the musical and other programs on MTV help them define who they are and how they will interact with others during the difficult transition

1. Survey of Americans on HIV/AIDS by the Henry J. Kaiser Family Foundation, March 24–April 18.

period from childhood to adulthood. MTV follows its audience's interests in creating its programming, and it has found that its viewers are at an age when they are becoming interested in sex and exploring their own sexuality. Youth under the age of 25 make up more than half of new HIV infections worldwide, making them vital actors in the fight against its spread. Reflecting this interest, MTV has created programming that teaches its viewers about the importance of testing for HIV and other sexually transmitted infections, monogamy, and correct condom use and encourages open dialogue about safe sex with their partners.

MTV and other media outlets are in a prime position to influence the actions of their viewers. Around the world, as young people are trying to figure out what kind of adults they will become, they tend to emulate the actors, athletes, musicians, and other celebrities they see on television. In its AIDS-related programming, MTV takes advantage of the position of celebrities as role models to provide positive images. While its viewers are copying the fashion, language, and styles of their favorite celebrities, it is hoped that they will also copy their appreciation for good sexual health. In other words, when young people see the people they look up to, admire, and consider sexy advocating for safe sex and other methods of preventing HIV infection, they are more likely to see safe sex as an attractive option for themselves than if they hear the same messages from adults with whom they have a harder time identifying. In fact, MTV Japan is explicitly trying to make safe sex "sexy" to young people with its slogan "be sexy, be safe."

As noted above, MTV is a part of the Viacom media conglomerate, which has also formed a partnership with the Henry J. Kaiser Family Foundation to leverage its access to large segments of the population to spread messages in support of prevention and against stigma and discrimination. The K**NO**W HIV/AIDS campaign includes PSAs, television and radio programming, and free print and online content. A broad range of television shows on Viacom networks have dealt with the subject of HIV/AIDS by weaving AIDS-related themes into their storylines. By combining such programming with PSAs, the networks are able to teach people explicitly about HIV/AIDS and then reinforce that teaching more informally through less "preachy" means.

MTV was at the forefront of this effort when it included a character with AIDS in its reality program *The Real World*. Launched in 1992, the program became one of the first popular reality television shows in the United States and pioneered a path for other reality shows to follow. The show's 1994 season took place in San Francisco and featured an openly gay man with AIDS, Pedro Zamora, at a time when few people with AIDS were willing to reveal their status publicly. Zamora's participation in the show gave young people around the country a window into the real-life challenges of a person living with AIDS and personalized the illness for many people. Zamora was already a vocal advocate for AIDS awareness when he joined the *Real World* cast, providing testimony before Congress about the importance of providing information about HIV/AIDS to young people in language they can relate to, something MTV itself was trying to do. Throughout the show, Zamora educated his fellow cast members on AIDS, and audiences around the country saw the other members grow in their understanding of the disease and in their acceptance of Zamora as a human being and friend, regardless of his HIV status. Following Zamora's death—the day after the last episode of the season was aired—President Bill Clinton praised his efforts and noted that his appearance on the reality show meant that all of its viewers could now say that they "knew" someone with AIDS.

Decision-Making Process

The decision for MTV to engage in the fight against HIV/AIDS was a very natural one. When the world first began to learn about the disease, it was spreading primarily in the gay community, which is well represented in the entertainment industry. Today, more than half of all new HIV infections are in young people, who make up MTV's target audience. HIV infection is spread primarily through sexual contact, and MTV's audience is at an age when they are becoming interested in sex and beginning to explore their own sexuality. Therefore, it only makes sense for MTV to offer them programming on safe sex so that they can protect themselves.

In developing its programming, MTV made an important decision to get involved where it can make a difference. Its comparative advantage was reaching large numbers of young people and keeping their attention. For that reason, it decided to focus its efforts on behavior and attitudinal change rather than, for example, support for treatment.

Leadership

MTV Networks International Chairman and CEO Bill Roedy has been an active spokesperson for AIDS. He has a strong personal and professional interest in AIDS, having personally lost friends to the disease. He also recognizes that AIDS is taking a toll on MTV's employees and viewers, and it therefore makes good business sense to deal with its spread. In 1998, he served as an ambassador for UNAIDS, and he served as the chair of the Global Business Coalition on HIV and AIDS from 2000 to 2002. In 2005, UN Secretary-General Kofi Annan appointed him as chair of the Global Media AIDS Initiative. Every year, Mr. Roedy goes on a field trip—unrelated to his regular business—so that he can meet with young people who are at the forefront of the epidemic. The people he meets inspire him and have shown him the positive side of the disease: the passionate people who are working hard to make a difference and to change mindsets.

At the same time, he has several staff who are working on HIV/AIDS-related issues full time, something the vice president of public affairs considers one of the company's advantages in its AIDS-related activities. This arrangement allows the president to put a strong public face on the company's fight against HIV/AIDS without having to spend too much of his limited business time on it.

Impact and Challenges for the Company

One clear impact of its strong commitment to HIV/AIDS-related programming is the positive publicity it creates for MTV. The contribution that the company is making—particularly to reaching young audiences, which are relatively difficult for other actors to reach—is widely acknowledged. The network is often accused of encouraging young people to have sex as a result of the fairly explicit nature of much of its general programming. However, since the content is driven by its viewers' interests, it has found that its role is to make sure that the messages its viewers are getting about sex prominently feature safe sex.

An additional positive impact is employee morale. MTV employees are proud of the fact that their employer really cares about these issues and is taking action rather than just talking about it. Many MTV employees ask how they can get involved in HIV/AIDS-related work, and once they are involved they try to stay involved.

One challenge to MTV is finding ways to remain creative and constantly come up with new ways of presenting what is essentially the same information so that it still jumps out at its viewers. MTV viewers are interested in the cutting edge, and it is difficult to keep young audiences interested in the same message over a sustained period of time without constantly rethinking the way in which it is presented.

Interviews

Georgia Arnold, Vice President, Public Affairs, MTV Networks International

Stephen Massey, Senior Program Officer, Entertainment Media Partnerships, Henry J. Kaiser Family Foundation

About JCIE and the FGFJ

Japan Center for International Exchange

Founded in 1970, the Japan Center for International Exchange (JCIE) is one of the few independent nongovernmental organizations in the field of international affairs in Japan. It conducts programs of exchange, research, and dialogue that bring together key figures from diverse sectors of society in Japan and overseas. JCIE conducts programs in the following three areas:

Global ThinkNet
Promoting analysis and discussion of critical issues facing Japan, Asia Pacific, and the global community in cooperation with leading institutions and scholars around the world.

Political Exchange Program
Encouraging Japanese and overseas leaders to exchange views on pressing security, economic, and foreign policy issues in order to promote mutual understanding and foster greater cooperation.

CivilNet
Strengthening the philanthropic and nonprofit sectors in Japan, Asia, and worldwide; promoting research and dialogue on civil society; and encouraging cooperation on shared domestic and international challenges.

Friends of the Global Fund, Japan

The Friends of the Global Fund, Japan (FGFJ), was created as a private support group for the Global Fund to Fight AIDS, Tuberculosis and Malaria in March 2004. The board consists of experts from various sectors and is co-chaired by prominent members of Japan's two main political parties—Motohisa Furukawa of the Democratic Party of Japan and Ichiro Aisawa of the Liberal Democratic Party. The FGFJ aims to create an enabling environment in Japan for an effective response to fight against the spread of HIV/AIDS and other communicable diseases. At the same time, it seeks to encourage Japan to expand its role in the battle against communicable diseases and build cooperation between Japan and other Asian countries in this shared struggle. JCIE serves as secretariat for the FGFJ.